LIFE IN THE AGE OF CHIVALRY

LIFE

IN THE

AGE OF
CHIVALRY

Published by

THE READER'S DIGEST ASSOCIATION LIMITED

London   New York   Sydney
Montreal   Cape Town

METALWORK
Silversmiths beat
metal on an anvil to
form a thin sheet.

TRANSPORT In the Middle Ages wagons for conveying people became covered and horses began to replace oxen.

LIFE IN THE AGE OF CHIVALRY

Edited and designed by Toucan Books Limited

Sole author: Nick Yapp

First edition copyright © 1993

The Reader's Digest Association Limited,

11 Westferry Circus, Canary Wharf, London E14 4HE

Reprinted 1999

Copyright © 1993

Reader's Digest Association Far East Limited

Philippines copyright © 1993

Reader's Digest Association Far East Limited

All rights reserved

Printing and binding:

Printer Industria Gráfica S.A, Barcelona

Separations: J Film Process Limited, Bangkok, Thailand

Paper: Perigord-Condat, France

ISBN 0 276 42122 1

ROMANCE
Lovers exchange
rings in 15th-
century France.

Front cover (clockwise from top left): Musician
with drum; knights jousting; 15th-century
pilgrim's badge; 15th-century song sheet; street
traders in 15th-century France; musicians playing
on steps of cathedral; statue of Sire de Coucy.
Back cover: 14th-century French banquet; silver-
gilt drinking cup; Great Domesday Book; castle
under siege; French jeweller's shop; a merchant's
clerk; halberd, used by foot soldiers.
Page 1: Harrowing in the 14th century. The man on
the left is attempting to kill the crows flying
overhead with his sling.
Pages 2 and 3: The Burgundian Court in the 15th
century celebrates at a festival to rival those of the
king of France.

CONTENTS

HOUSEWORK
Sweeping a floor, a 15th-century illustration.

MAN AT WORK
A craftsman working on the rim of a bowl; an illustration from an Italian document.

SHOPPING
A customer waits while the shopkeeper weighs dried meat on a hand-held balance.

FARMER A peasant sows while his dog scares away a crow.

KNOWING YOUR PLACE

Everyone had his or her place in the elaborate structure of medieval society. From the pope,

emperor or king down to the humblest serf, the interlocking pieces of the feudal system created an

edifice which allowed many brutalities, but also magnificent flowerings of the arts, trade and culture.

I N EUROPE the Middle Ages were a time of considerable contradictions: between wealth and poverty, famine and plenty, ignorance and learning, reason and superstition. In general, standards of living improved between the 10th and 15th centuries and people ate better at the end of the period than at the beginning; but there were years when the whole of Europe starved, and people were reported to be eating the bodies of criminals hanging from gibbets.

Men raised magnificent cathedrals to the glory of God and yet Christian armies slaughtered each other in battle. Armed mercenaries held towns, cities and whole regions to ransom. In the east, the armies of the Ottoman Empire passed through Greece and Serbia, along the banks of the Danube, until they threatened the heart of Europe. In the west, the Christian kings of Spain struggled for centuries to drive the Moors out of Andalusia. In the centre, France and England were intermittently at war for over 100 years.

And yet, at the same time, trade routes opened all over the continent and beyond. Trains of packhorses, asses and mules carried barrels of wine, suits of armour, bales of cloth and fleeces of raw wool from the Channel to the Black Sea, from the Aegean to the Atlantic. Arab caravans brought silks, cottons and spices from the Middle East; and ships from the Baltic exported fish and timber to England, France and Spain and on to the Mediterranean.

Travel was slow. It took at least nine days for a merchant to send goods from Venice to Naples (only 460 miles away), 27 days to send goods to London, and 46 days to reach Lisbon.

In an age when horizons were limited and most people rarely, if ever, left the villages in which they were born, some were bold enough to investigate the rest of the world. Within a period of little over 200 years, the Italian Marco Polo had crossed Asia on an overland route to China (between 1270 and 1295);

Pêro de Covilhã had explored the west coast of Africa as far south as Sierra Leone in the early 1440s; Bartholomew Diaz had rounded the Cape of Good Hope at the southern tip of Africa in the late 1480s; Christopher Columbus had 'discovered' a New World in 1492; and Vasco da Gama had found a sea route to India five years later. And, with each voyage, each discovery, came new wealth and new trade – in pepper, perfume, carpets, jewels, spices, porcelain, slaves, and gold and silver.

PUSHING BACK THE FRONTIERS

Repeated outbreaks of plague destroyed hundreds of communities across Europe. At the same time, however, towns and cities arose with towering cathedrals, fine houses, guild and market halls that flaunted the wealth of the trades that built them. Universities were founded in Paris and Padua, Oxford and Cambridge, Salamanca and Valladolid, Naples and Bologna. Outside these centres of learning and commerce lay a countryside that was steadily being hacked from the wild. Huge forests in the Ardennes in northern France and southern Italy were still impenetrable. The peaks of the Pyrenees and the Apennines, the Balkans and the Carpathians were unconquered and unknown. Bears, wild boars and wolves roamed freely over most of Europe, but the land was slowly coming under cultivation.

Throughout Europe, society was controlled by the feudal system. All land was said to belong to God but, as God's agents on earth, rulers could manage it and dispose of it as they wished. Kings could therefore grant land to others – their nobles and knights – men who had performed well in battle, or saved the king's life. These men, in turn, could grant smaller tracts of land to their faithful freemen. All landowners, however, owed allegiance to their superiors: in return for the land they had been given, they had to render services – either a number of days' work a year on their lord's land, or the raising and equipping of a

FEUDAL SYSTEM   An illustration in a 14th-century French manuscript shows the hierarchy of medieval society. The French king and German emperor are attended by church dignitaries, soldiers and servants.

certain number of armed men to fight for their lord. The authority of the lord was absolute; it was he who decided what work was to be done and when.

In theory, the feudal system created a solid, immovable social pyramid, with the king at the top and, at the bottom, villeins and bondmen who owned no land and had to pay (in rent and service) for the right to farm an acre or two. Those at the bottom of the pyramid did as they were told, under pain of severe punishment, and respected the privileges of the lord. Hawking was a noble pastime, but not one for churls (peasants). Any villein who found a lost hawk and failed to return it to its owner had to bare his breast while the bird ate 6 ounces of his flesh. With

good luck, hard work, good health and good management, however, it was possible to ascend the pyramid. There were plenty of poor knights who found wealth and favour with their king by some feat of arms on the battlefield and then capitalised on this promotion by marrying into rich families.

There were aspiring clerics who found employment with bishop or archbishop, and then themselves rose to the highest positions in the Church, living in palaces that often rivalled royal residences. And there were humble yeoman farmers who steadily increased their holdings of land, acquired large estates by marriage and eventually achieved noble status. There were also those whose fortunes waned: noble families who had fallen on hard times, or who had forfeited their estates through acts of treason – which often amounted to backing the wrong side during a civil war; and knights whose land yielded little and who were landlords to only a few miserable peasants.

THE HAND OF GOD

What was common to all, wherever they lived, was the Church's immediate and daily presence. People saw God's handiwork in everything around – except those sinister events that they regarded as the work of the devil. A plentiful harvest and good health were signs of God's love and approval: a poor harvest, a flood, a fire or a visit from the plague were proof of God's punishment for sin, or heresy.

Nevertheless, old pagan festivals were still celebrated side by side with the feast days of the Christian saints. People prayed to God for relief from their pain, illness and disease, but they also sought more immediate help in the cures and spells of folklore and sorcery. To be baptised in a church and buried in consecrated church ground was essential for salvation but, between these two events, life was dominated by a mixture of superstition and faith.

THE CHURCH IN SOCIETY A choir of Dominican nuns sings at Mass in the chapel of their convent (above). A priest on horseback makes his pilgrimage to Canterbury (right).

War Games A 15th-century tournament (above), where armed knights practise their battle skills at the joust. A lady (right) receives news of the death of her knight, whose shield is brought by a servant.

All men needed some skill in arms. Even if they were never called to the battlefield, there were plunderers and robbers, outlaws and marauding bands, against whom they had to defend home and land. It was the duty of every knight to learn how to fight with two-handed sword, lance, dagger, battle-axe or mace. Yeomen and peasants were encouraged or ordered to practise their skills with longbow, cross-bow or pike. Even the clergy bore arms, though the Church forbade them to 'smite with the edge of the sword' (many eased their consciences by using instead a club-headed mace with ridged edges).

The Middle Ages were the great age of the castle – at first, little more than a fortified hilltop surrounded by a wooden fence and perhaps a shallow ditch, later an elaborate defence system of towers and battlements, keeps and courtyards that housed hundreds of fighting men and their families. They were also the age of the tournament, which started as rough and ready free-for-alls, but became contests of single combat, where knights honed their skills as mounted fighters, competing for the approval of a prince or the favour of a lady. After one tournament, a group of knights found William the

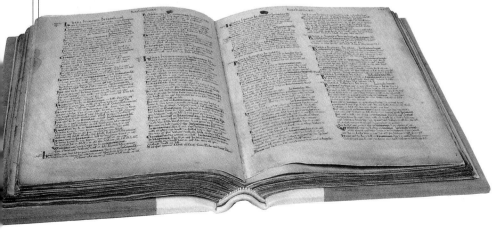

Great Domesday Book Nearly 20 years after the Norman Conquest, King William ordered a survey of all lands, livestock, rents and people in England. The result was the Domesday Book.

WORK AND PLAY   A leisurely game of chess (left) in 15th-century France contrasts with the hard labours of a ploughman (above).

Marshal, a 12th-century English warrior, in the local smithy, with his head on the anvil, having his helmet hammered back into shape so that he could get it off his head.

CONFLICTING DEMANDS

Nowhere is the contradictory nature of the age better epitomised than in the demands made of a knight. On the one hand, he was to be fearless in battle. On the other hand, he was to be gentle, courteous, devout, generous and cultured. In a 12th-century manuscript, a cleric named John of Salisbury listed some of these knightly duties: 'To defend the Church, to assail infidelity, to venerate the priesthood, to protect the poor from injuries … to pour out his blood for his

brothers (as the formula of his oath directs him) …' When the knight rode out, he carried much responsibility upon his well-armoured shoulders. These, then, were the men who dominated the medieval battlefield for hundreds of years, until the invention of gunpowder and the forging of cannon brought this domination, and the age of chivalry itself, to an end.

In 1500 there were only five cities in the whole of Europe with more than 100,000 inhabitants: Paris, Venice, Naples, Milan and Constantinople. Nine out of every ten people lived in tiny villages and worked on the land. Children learnt at an early age how to scare birds from the fields, pick stones off the land, and collect wild berries and nuts from the woods that surrounded most settlements. They watched their mothers and grandmothers tending geese and chickens, often while spinning yarn from the distaff that the women carried with them. They learnt how to scatter seed evenly over the newly ploughed earth, and a few months later they struggled to help to gather in the harvest. That was their pattern of life from year to year, from infancy to the grave; that was how they spent their lives in the same village.

The routine of daily life remained much the same throughout the Middle Ages, but there were improve-

KNOWING THEIR PLACE The magistrate works for the lord of the manor and receives the farmers, who are here to pledge their continuing allegiance.

ments that made life a little easier. One of the greatest of all was the appearance around the 11th century of the heavy-wheeled mouldboard plough, a machine that not only cut a furrow through the soil, but also turned it with the blade of the mouldboard, bringing the richer bottom soil to the top of the furrow – 'thus it be cleansed and rid of the water the which maketh the tillage good', wrote Walter of Henley, a 13th-century English expert on agriculture.

The development of the mouldboard plough was a simple change, but it resulted in far greater yields of wheat and rye, barley and oats. It probably improved the quality of life for more people in the Middle Ages than any other invention.

There were other great technological advances, including the invention of the compass, the mechanical clock, the spinning wheel, the treadle loom and spectacles. Glass gradually replaced sheets of parchment or pieces of oiled cloth in the windows of houses. There were also inventions that removed some of the backbreaking physical labour from daily work – the windmill and the watermill.

As people learnt to harness the power of wind and water more effectively, hundreds of thousands of windmills and water-mills were built all over Europe. Windmills were used primarily to grind corn. Watermills were more versatile; water power was used to drive massive hammers in forges and to tan leather, as well as grind corn. The millers themselves, however, were often mistrusted: 'What is the boldest thing in the village?' inquired one popular peasant riddle. 'A miller's shirt,' was the answer, 'for it grips a thief by the throat every day.'

For a period that is often portrayed as brutal and insensitive, the Middle Ages saw the flowering of many of the arts: music, painting, sculpture. Many of its great buildings and residences were treasure troves of ornament and ostentation. Princes and prelates rivalled each other in magnificent displays of their wealth – in palaces and formal gardens, in a piece of jewellery or a tapestry, in the uniforms of their retainers, and often in magnificent banquets, where the food served could include anything from larks to vultures. When the English Prince Lionel, Duke of Clarence, married Violante Visconti in Milan in 1368, the bride's father (the ruler of Milan) bestowed rich gifts on his 1500 followers. They included coats of armour for the men and their horses, richly woven surcoats embroidered with gems, greyhounds in velvet collars, and enamelled bottles of fine wine.

THE BASIS OF SOCIETY A stained-glass scene of the Biblical characters Sarah and Tobias in bed symbolises domestic contentment and implies that faith in God will be rewarded.

FAMILY VALUES

The bedrock of medieval society was the family. Children were brought up in strict obedience to the laws of state and Church, as well as to the wishes of their parents. Husbands and wives stayed together for life, and, despite the fact that their marriages were usually arranged for them, there is much evidence of marital devotion, as well as duty. In December 1441, Margaret Paston, pregnant with her first child, wrote from Oxnead in Norfolk to her husband, John, in London. 'Right reverend and worshipful husband, I recommend me to you, desiring heartily to hear of your welfare ... I pray that you will wear the ring with the image of St Margaret that I sent you for a remembrance till you come home; you have left me such a remembrance that makes me think upon you both day and night when I would sleep ...'

As the 10th century drew to a close and the second millennium approached, one Frankish monk recorded that 'the world is growing old: we live at the end of time.' He was not alone in this fear – there were many who believed that the world was about to end. Even when the millennium passed without catastrophe, there were those who saw terrifying portents in every thunderstorm and earthquake, flash flood and drought, battle and outbreak of plague, or in the baying of wolves in the forests at night. Medieval Europe survived, however, to change and develop into the Renaissance.

LIFE IN THE MEDIEVAL FAMILY

Wives obeyed their husbands; children obeyed their parents.

The medieval family was a unit of strict control at all levels of society.

With so many children dying in infancy, those who survived were all the more valued.

Young children were indulged with toys and games, from rag dolls to spinning tops.

But – around the age of seven – they were put to work on the land or

sent to be trained in knightly ways at the castle of a local lord.

COURTSHIP AND MARRIAGE

Few medieval marriages started as love affairs – for all but the poor, marriages were

arranged by the parents of bride and groom. Courtship was formal or non-existent.

Weddings were costly and elaborate, and divorce was unknown.

PERCEIVED FROM the present, the Middle Ages were a period of massive contradictions – and in no aspect of everyday life was this more true than in the rituals of the family and the relationships between men and women. On the one hand, marriage was a fairly mercenary matter, with the property drive considerably more powerful than the sex drive in forming attachments. On the other, the notion – at least – of romantic love was extremely popular among the aristocracy.

For rich and poor alike, life in the Middle Ages centred around the family, of which the senior male member was always undisputed head. Christianity did not improve the traditional subjugation of the female sex, since the Western Church held women – in the form of Eve – to be responsible for the downfall of man. Most women, therefore, had to struggle to achieve any sort of status.

Even the legal status of the married woman was decidedly inferior to that of any free man. Although she was responsible for her own actions, she could not enter into contracts on her own behalf; her husband was responsible for all her debts; her personal goods were her husband's property and, if she inherited any property or land, its use belonged to him.

For the nobles, marriage was the means of establishing a legitimate line of succession; it was also at the heart of most medieval diplomacy as a source of land and alliances. For townsmen, marriage could provide commercially attractive unions with other trading families. And for peasants, marriage meant children who, in turn, could provide cheap labour on the land – though too many could mean less food to go around.

People generally preferred sons because, in most parts of Europe, the property of a man who died without a male heir was divided equally among his daughters. This diminished the wealth and power of the family. Winter was considered better than summer for conceiving males, and various tell-tale signs were said to indicate a son: a clear and fresh complexion in a pregnant woman, for example, or a greater swelling of the left breast.

A DUCAL COURT
Lodovico Gonzaga, a 15th-century ruler of Mantua, and Barbara, his wife, with members of their court.

HIGH SPIRITS A mischievous guest plants his foot on the bridal train at a Burgundian wedding in 1462.

Marrying for love was almost unknown. For the rich it was often a business arrangement; and for a serf it was often compulsory, ordered by the lord of the manor. For example, in 1274, the Abbot of Hales in the English county of Lancashire ruled that: 'John of Romsley and Nicholas Sewal are given till next court to decide as to the widows offered them.' In much the same way, women who were wards of the king, or whose hand in marriage was in the gift of the king, had little say in who was chosen as their husband.

THE AGE OF THE ARRANGED MARRIAGE

Courtship in the modern sense of the word was almost non-existent. There was love within marriage, but seldom love before marriage. In the villages, future husbands and wives probably knew each other before their marriage was arranged, but among the rich, it was not thought necessary for young people to meet until their wedding day. In 1360, King Jean II of France effectively sold his 11-year-old daughter Isabelle in marriage to the son of the rich Visconti

family of Milan for 600,000 florins. There was nothing unusual in this, though the speed of the transaction (less than two months) was exceptional – Jean desperately needed the dowry. Marriage among most sections of the European population involved property. An heiress or widow could bring her land to her husband for his lifetime; where the wife had no land to bring, her relatives would provide a dowry of money and goods which would then become the property of the groom or his parents. In return, they would be expected to settle on the couple a 'jointure' – lands which remained with the wife for her lifetime. In any case, the wife would be entitled on her husband's death to a third of his estates for life. Thus, negotiations over a marriage often centred upon the exact balance of dowry and jointure, and hard bargaining was probably the rule. Among the peasants in rural areas throughout Europe it was the custom for friends or relatives of the male suitor to act as go-betweens – or for the village priest to arrange marriages between his parishioners. In southern France and Spain, a young man spent more time and money wooing his future mother-in-law than his bride. Any daughter who rejected her parents' choice was made to suffer. In her late teens, Elizabeth Paston of Norfolk refused to marry Stephen Scrope, a 50-year-old widower who admitted he was 'disfigured in my person and shall be while I live'. Elizabeth's

BETROTHAL A barefoot labourer attends an Anglo-Saxon wedding. A painted shield (right) shows a knight offering his armour to his lady.

COURTLY LOVE

Suffering for the love of an unattainable woman was the theme of much medieval poetry, and became a model of knightly behaviour.

UNLESS THEY JOINED the Church, young men of noble or knightly birth in the Middle Ages were expected to enjoy fighting, with all its blood and gore. But as the period progressed, they also came to see themselves more and more as the polished pinnacles of society. For the aspiring knight this posed a problem: was he to be a doughty fighter, or a well-mannered gentleman, tempering skill at arms with humility and grace?

One solution to this dilemma was offered by the evolution of a knightly ideal, a composite of three medieval concepts: courtliness, courtesy and courtly love. Courtliness was a code of manners that established rules for correct behaviour at court. It evolved in the courts of France, Flanders and the Holy Roman Empire from the mid-11th century onwards. Courtesy was more of an ideal, defining the qualities required of a knight: compassion, shame (which for people in the Middle Ages included a reverence for others' rights and needs), generosity, humility, beauty (of thought and action), nobility, moderation, good breeding, leadership, manliness coupled with a cheerful disposition, and mastery of arms. Like courtliness, courtesy was not solely a

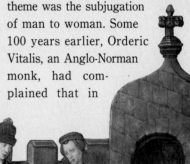

EXQUISITE PAIN A couple languish in the garden of love.

European invention. Much the same ideals were found in Islamic teaching.

Courtly love, however, was confined to Europe. It originated in the works of a handful of German poets, writing in the later 12th and early 13th centuries. One of the greatest of its exponents was Wolfram von Eschenbach, author of *Parzival*, an epic poem telling the story of a young man, brought up by his widowed mother in ignorance of the military adventures of his father. As he grows up, he begins to question his role in life, seeking understanding of the duties of a knight. He wanders the countryside for five years, meeting pilgrims, knights and a hermit, all of whom help him in his quest. He arrives at the court of the mythical King Arthur, has many adventures and comes to realise the true meaning of knightly valour.

Among Eschenbach's pupils was Walther von der Vogelweide, and these two, with Konrad

GARDEN OF LOVE In courtly love romances, the lover often enters the garden where his love resides through a locked door.

von Wurzburg and Wolfgang of Erlau (author of the *Nibelungenlied*, the saga of the knight Siegfried), defined the concept of courtly love.

Reinmar von Hagenau, another of von der Vogelweide's teachers and rivals, captured the essence of courtly love in a *minnesang*, or love lyric:

*I wish to be known my entire life as a
master of one thing and one thing only;
I seek the world's praise for this one
skill,
That no man can bear his suffering as
beautifully as I.
If a woman causes me pain to such an
extent that
I cannot remain silent night or day,
I have so gentle a spirit that I'll accept
her hate as a source of joy;
And yet, alas, how deeply that
discomforts me!*

Courtly love was thus a literary creation, whose exquisite fantasies would not necessarily have borne much relation to real life. Its main theme was the subjugation of man to woman. Some 100 years earlier, Orderic Vitalis, an Anglo-Norman monk, had complained that in

GOLDEN CHAINS A lady binds the hands of her lover to symbolise their mutual love. Left: A German knight of the 13th century in full regalia.

For more than 100 years the ideals of courtly love flourished in the literature written to entertain aristocratic society in medieval Europe. Indeed, modern concepts of the medieval knight as the perfect gentleman, motivated by heroism and love, stem from the 13th century.

By the end of the 13th century, however, its influence declined. The Italian poet Dante came to condemn courtly love. The Spaniard Cervantes mocked it in his *Don Quixote*. A later German poet, Neidhart von Reuenthal, wrote poems in which he presented his knightly hero as a man irresistible to village lasses. Writers increasingly questioned the idea that love could be ennobling or distinguished from simple lust. The age of courtly love was over.

'their vain and novel customs of dress and personal culture' many knights aimed solely at pleasing women. The implication was that knights were neglecting their duties to God and their lords, when they concerned themselves with purely amorous adventures. It was now held that a true knight should spend his life in a state of unrequited love, worshipping a woman whom he could never hope to win and suffering exquisite agony in the process.

ALL FOR LOVE In the allegory *The Book of the Heart Possessed by Love,* Cueur (the heart possessed by love) is pushed into the Stream of Tears by the Black Knight (symbolising trouble) and Lady Hope tries to rescue him.

LIFE IN THE MEDIEVAL FAMILY

cousin wrote to her brother: 'Since Easter she [Elizabeth] has been mostly beaten once or twice a week and sometimes twice in one day, and her head broken in two or three places.' But poor Elizabeth won in the end: negotiations with Scrope were terminated.

Child marriages were confined to the wealthy and the aristocratic. The 12th-century *Life of St Hugh of Lincoln*, for example, tells of a young girl thrice married and twice widowed before she was 11 years old. In the latter half of the 12th century, Pope Alexander II decreed that the minimum age for marriage should be 14 for the groom and 12 for the bride. Although children as young as seven could be betrothed, their marriage only became legal once it had been consummated at a later date.

In the later Middle Ages, formal marriages always took place in church, but many countries had also for a long time recognised the validity of a union consisting of a couple who lived together with the intention of becoming man and wife. In a 12th-century study of canon law, Gratian, a monk and lawyer from Bologna in Italy, noted that 'a young couple lustful but maritally affectionate should not be called fornicators, but spouses'. All that was needed was that the couple state that they took each other as man and wife.

Although this rule remained until the Reformation, the Church steadily tightened its control over marriage. In 1215 the decree *Cum Inhibitio* of Pope Innocent III made the publication of banns a general law of the Western Church, and confirmed earlier prohibitions against clandestine marriages. In the same year, in England, the *Magna Carta* of King John laid down that marriage of royal wards should be without 'disparagement' – that is, it should only be between persons of equal social standing.

Weddings were times of such public celebration, but also sometimes scandal, that it is hardly surprising that Bishop Poore, writing in England in 1223, ordered that marriages 'be celebrated reverently and with honour, not with laughter or sport, or in taverns or at public potations or feasts'. This did not deter the rich. In 1468 Margaret, the sister of King Edward IV of England, married Charles, Duke of Burgundy – ruler of the most cultured court north of the Alps.

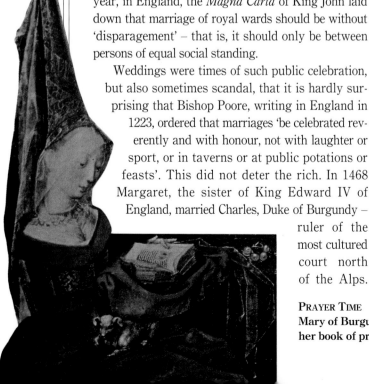

PRAYER TIME
Mary of Burgundy reads her book of prayers.

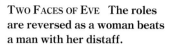

TWO FACES OF EVE The roles are reversed as a woman beats a man with her distaff.

At the reception there were pageants on the theme of marriage, Adam and Eve, and the feast of Cana. But it was the duke's courtly displays rather than the municipal celebrations that made the most impression: the men dressed as animals; the nine days of jousting and feasting which followed the marriage, with the tables covered by gold tissue and lit by chandeliers; and the duke himself, riding to the jousts with clothes and horses encrusted with jewels.

DIVORCE AND DEATH

In theory, there was no such thing as divorce in the Middle Ages. Couples sometimes separated – usually when the husband turned the wife out of the matrimonial home. And a marriage could be annulled if it was unconsummated, or on the grounds that it had not been valid in the first place. But only the pope himself could put man and wife asunder, and there had to be sound political or commercial reasons for His Holiness to act.

For the vast majority, only death could end a marriage. Because then, as now, women tended to live longer than men (and so many men were killed at war), there was a surplus of widows. In many ways, however, the life of a widow was better than that of a wife – particularly since medieval husbands were occasionally encouraged by clerics to beat and kick their wives. The widow often became head of the household. Her private rights in law became the same as a man's and she had absolute rights in her own property, including the large share of her husband's goods left to her; she also had a minimum of a third of her husband's estates for life. Her position on the marriage market suddenly became extremely strong and second – and sometimes third and fourth – marriages were common. In some countries, laws had to be passed to restrict a widow's right to remarry, on the grounds that there were not enough men to go round. A woman who remarried within a year of her previous husband's death lost all right to the property she

MARRIAGE PORTRAIT   Jan van Eyck's painting of 1434 provides a glimpse into the Bruges home of the merchant Giovanni Arnolfini.

DIVIDED LOYALTIES: THE DE COUCY FAMILY

MOST KINGS AND PRINCES had to be prepared to fight on two fronts during the Middle Ages. They had to defend their frontiers from their neighbours; and they had to fight to establish effective control over their own territory. Feudalism decreed that all men owed allegiance to their lord, but few rulers could take that for granted. The more powerful a local lord, the more his loyalty had to be wooed.

For 400 years, from the late 10th century, no king of France could assume the support of the arrogant de Coucy family. From a secure base in Picardy, the Sires de Coucy became some of the most successful practitioners of the medieval local war. They conducted their affairs as though they were princes.

DIVIDED HEART A plaque on the tomb of Enguerrand VII, last of the de Coucy line, displays his family's arms. Right: The Sire de Coucy rides forth.

They had their own courts of justice, coined their own money, raised their own taxes and maintained a private army. They employed their own physicians, priests, painters, astrologers, secretaries, jesters and servants: the resident staff at the de Coucy chateau alone numbered over 500 souls. Such men could command a high price for their support.

Kings of France carefully monitored the marriages and alliances formed by the de Coucys with other families. Despite attempts by the French monarch to control the de Coucys, the family continued to build their wealth and power. By the 14th century they owned estates in England, too – in Yorkshire and Lancashire, Westmorland and Cumberland. Enguerrand VII, the last

of the de Coucy line, was created Earl of Bedford after marrying the over-indulged Isabella, daughter of Edward III of England. This posed the problem of a truly divided loyalty since, for much of Enguerrand's life, England and France were engaged in the Hundred Years' War. On the one hand, he owed allegiance for his English lands to his father-in-law; on the other, to his natural overlord, the king of France. As his friends argued – when a sense of nationhood was first developing in both France and England – he was French 'by name, blood and extraction'.

Enguerrand professed neutrality or, when the occasion demanded, went off to fight in campaigns that were not directed against the English. Finally, however, a decision had to be made. In his renunciation of the English half of his forked allegiance, he wrote to the new English king, Richard II: 'Now that it has happened that war has arisen between my natural and sovereign lord, on the one part, and you on the other ... I grieve more than at anything.' Part of his grief, perhaps, was caused by the fact that in choosing a nationality he was renouncing not just his allegiance and his fellowship in the Order of the Garter but also his wife and English lands.

When Enguerrand died – captured on a Crusade – in a Turkish prison, the French part of the de Coucy domain was, much to the relief of the king of France, eventually acquired by the French Crown.

PROUD MAN
'I am the Sire de Coucy,' proclaims this 19th-century statuette.

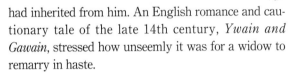

FAMILY LIFE
Bringing up children was the woman's responsibility alone. Right: A housewife of the 14th century receives a love letter in a casket, most probably from her husband.

had inherited from him. An English romance and cautionary tale of the late 14th century, *Ywain and Gawain*, stressed how unseemly it was for a widow to remarry in haste.

CHIVALRY AND COURTLY LOVE

Although trained primarily for war, medieval knights were expected to abide by a code of chivalry. From the Danube to the Atlantic this moral system went far beyond mere bravery in combat. The bedrock of chivalry was loyalty to lord or king, but on top of this were rules which governed every aspect of a knight's behaviour – especially his attitude towards women.

The fables of King Arthur, and even the modern fantasies of Hollywood based on them, are not too farfetched. Knighthood was received in the name of the Holy Trinity, and a knight made a vow to place his sword at the service of justice, piety, the orphaned and the oppressed, the Church and the widow. In the words of a 15th-century Spanish writer, Diaz de Gámez, the knight should be 'wary and prudent, continent and temperate, enduring and courageous'.

In the 12th century, the French Andreas Capellanus set down 31 Rules of Courtly Love, including:

Marriage is no real excuse for not loving.
It is not proper to love any woman whom one
   would be ashamed to seek to marry.
When made public, love rarely endures.
A man in love is always apprehensive.
Nothing forbids one woman being loved by
   two men or one man by two women.

Courtly love has been described by historians as the 'dreamland' of chivalry. On the one hand, it was love as we understand it – romantic and free from sordid business arrangements. On the other hand, strictly interpreted, it was love for another man's wife – like the love of Sir Lancelot for Queen Guinevere in the tales of King Arthur.

This idealisation of an adulterous romance made the concept most appealing to those not bound by the chivalric code. Troubadours crossed Provence with their songs of passionate devotion, rejection and renewed wooing. *Minnesingers* walked the length and breadth of the Holy Roman Empire with their songs and verses that told of desire, deeds of valour and secret love. In reality such liaisons often ended in tragedy, though never quite as macabre as in the romance of the *Châtelain de Coucy*, which was written in the middle of the 14th century.

In this masterpiece of 8266 lines of verse, a knight is fatally wounded by a poisoned arrow while on the Third Crusade. He writes a last letter to his lady, to be sent to her, together with his embalmed heart. The lady's husband intercepts heart and letter, and has the former cooked and served to his wife.

In terms of courtly love, however, the tale has a most satisfactory ending. The lady swears that she will never eat again, and dies, while the husband goes on a lifelong pilgrimage. Love, death and melancholy are in perfect harmony. Such was the very essence of courtly love.

MEDIEVAL MUSIC

In this time of musical experiment, there emerged the forerunners of many of today's musical forms and instruments.

MEDIEVAL BRASS This trumpet, made in four parts, was found during excavations in the City of London. It probably dates from the 14th century.

THE MOST COMMON musical sound of the Middle Ages was the human voice raised in song. A variety of musical instruments existed, but their manufacture was a slow, complicated and expensive business, and their use was largely confined to the halls of kings or nobles.

Until the 11th century, all sacred and most secular singing was in unison – harmony was unknown. Choirs sang or chanted the praises of God in plainsong, always in the key of C, with all notes approximately the same length. Gradually, however, harmony was introduced, and with it the notion of embellishing or enlarging traditional pieces of music.

Composers also used improved systems of musical notation. At first notes were crudely written to show whether the pitch was to rise or fall. Once the five-line stave was introduced in the 12th century, written music became far more precise in indicating both the pitch and the length of a note.

As choirs became more skilled,

SONG SHEET A manuscript shows 15th-century music notation and monks playing musical instruments.

listening to music became more popular. On long winter evenings there was little entertainment to be had for rich or poor alike, and groups of singers were welcome wherever they went. People danced more often to a choir than a group of musicians. Troubadours and *minnesingers* (singers of love songs) wandered alone through the countryside, fitting their own music to ballads and poems, and accompanying themselves on fiddles or small harps. By the 13th century singing was one of only three subjects for scholarship examination at Winchester College – the other two were reading and Latin grammar.

OUTDOOR CONCERT An illustrated breviary (a combined prayer and hymn book) shows musicians playing on the steps of a Dutch cathedral.

SONG AND DANCE A dancer accompanies himself on a stringed instrument.

variety of instruments increased. The largest and loudest was the church organ, early examples of which date back to the 8th century.

There were two types of stringed instruments – those plucked and those played with a bow. The oldest was the harp, probably originating in Ireland. The psaltery was a cross between harp and guitar, with 32 strings tuned in pairs. The main bowed instruments were the rebec and the vielle, forerunners of the violin. Wind instruments included flutes, *shawms* (early forms of the oboe), trumpets and bagpipes.

People began to appreciate music more and more, though seldom with the reverent discipline associated with modern audiences. Music was really an accompaniment – to work or worship. And on at least one occasion it was used in battle – to drown the screams of the wounded and to frighten the enemy.

ARTS IN HARMONY Work began on St Mark's Cathedral, Venice, in 1042. It became a noted venue for the performance of sacred music.

At first, the main purpose of musical instruments was to imitate the sounds of nature – the songs of birds, the murmur of the wind, the ripple of running water. As techniques of musical instrument making improved, however, the range and

ANTIPHON A page from the 15th-century *Eton Choir Book* gives a chant in praise of the Virgin Mary.

MUSICAL INSTRUMENT
A 14th-century *gittern* with back, sides and neck carved from a single piece of wood.

THE PAINS OF CHILDBIRTH

The rejoicing that accompanied the birth of a baby was all too often followed

by a period of mourning for mother, child or both. A woman might endure many

pregnancies, but half her children were likely to die in infancy.

HE BIRTH of a child was usually a matter for great rejoicing, and it was just as well, for a healthy woman could expect to be pregnant between four and eight times during her life. This was partly because contraceptive methods were a mixture of optimism and superstition, little changed from the time of the ancient Greeks. Melted beeswax, egg-yolk, walnut leaves, saffron, onion, peppermint, dried roots, seaweed, rags, opium and grass were all used to block the mouth of the womb and thus prevent the entry of the sperm. Ignorance was, up to a point, the fault of the Church, which forbade contraception. It saw marriage as a second-best to chastity, insisting that sex take place only within marriage with the express purpose of procreation, and then only on certain days (from Monday to Thursday) when there was no special fast or festival.

The common form of birth control in the Middle Ages was almost certainly *coitus interruptus*, which was particularly condemned by the Church – commanding a penance of up to 10 years' fasting. There was also the belief then, as now, that a woman could not conceive while still nursing a baby. But the most effective form of contraception was malnutrition and overwork. How complex the ritual of childbirth was depended on the social standing of the mother-to-be.

In a peasant's cottage, arrangements were rough and ready. At court or in a castle, however, queens, princesses and noblewomen often took to their chamber six weeks before their confinement and then gave birth in public – to prevent allegations that the heir was a changeling.

It was very unusual throughout the medieval world for a father to be present at the birth of his child, for giving birth was considered a woman's affair. Indeed, one Italian writer, writing on the birth of twins or triplets, even advised that 'since this matter requires attention on the part of the woman there is no point in studying it at length.' Midwives (in the case of the rich) and female relatives (in the case of the poor) attended the lying-in chamber or the corner of the cottage where the baby was to be born. Nevertheless, there were some more enlightened medieval writings on the business of childbirth. In the 13th century, for example, the Italian Arnold of Villanova, in *De Regimine Sanitatis*, instructed midwives to make the early hours of a child's life as close to the conditions of the womb as possible – using gentle lights, quietness and soft blankets.

Childbirth was a time of peril for mother and baby alike. Since roughly five out of ten infants died within the first few years of life, and few people lived beyond 40, it is hardly surprising that many medieval writers stressed the sufferings of pregnancy and the mortal

CARRY-COTS A double pannier was carried across the shoulders; a vertical model strapped on the back.

THE PRICE OF LIFE

Because women were valued for bearing children, fines in early medieval France for killing one varied:

For killing a woman past child-bearing age
– 100 livres (pounds).

For killing a woman still of child-bearing age
– 200 livres.

For killing a pregnant woman – 700 livres.

READY FOR DELIVERY
A 15th-century man-
uscript shows four
of the positions a
foetus can take in
the womb.

risk of childbirth, and that pregnant women made their confession and received Holy Communion before labour. However, medical studies such as *De Passionibus Mulierum Curandarum* by Arnold of Villanova, were not short of instructions to midwives or relatives on delivery. If the baby presented itself other than head down, explained the treatise, the midwife was instructed to turn it by hand. She was also advised to tie a small bunch of the herb agrimony to the mother's thigh and to make her sneeze to speed the process.

Means of easing suffering were almost non-existent and, as in contraception, available help owed more to superstition than to knowledge. Women were taught chants and incantations or wore special amulets and birth girdles, which were handed down from generation to generation. And Jews, Muslims and Christians alike believed in the efficacy of semi-precious stones (usually an eaglestone) attached to the mother's thigh.

Once the mother had given birth, it was essential that she was 'churched'. For 40 days immediately after the birth – if

she could afford to – the mother stayed in her chamber. On the 41st day she was taken to church and, in a special service, cleansed of the impurity that was said to be within her.

PRIMARY CARE

Midwives or other attendants generally bathed the baby in warm water immediately after birth, swaddled it in a warm cloth, and then placed it in the mother's arms. There were more exotic instructions, however. To hasten healing, some people recommended that the end of the umbilical cord be rubbed with saliva, the ash of a snail, or cumin (a spice) and cicely (a herb). Trotula of Salerno recommended rubbing the baby's palate with honey and cleaning its tongue with hot water 'in order that it may speak more correctly'. The infant's ears 'must be pressed and shaped immediately and it must be done frequently'; and the limbs should be 'bound with a swaddling band' to straighten them. The worry was that an infant's flesh was

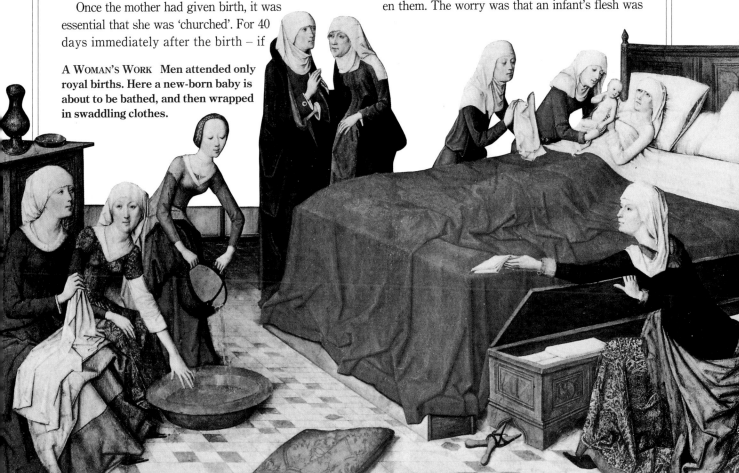

A WOMAN'S WORK Men attended only royal births. Here a new-born baby is about to be bathed, and then wrapped in swaddling clothes.

very pliable, and therefore in danger of becoming severely deformed.

Swaddling was practised throughout Europe, but less so in Wales and Ireland where infants were said to be 'abandoned to ruthless nature'. An anonymous 13th-century writer described the Welsh and Irish practice: 'They are not put in cradles or swathed; nor are their tender limbs helped by frequent baths or formed by any useful art.

'The midwives do not use hot water to raise the nose, or press down the face, or lengthen the legs. Unaided nature according to her own judgment arranges and disposes without the help of any art the limbs she has produced.' Despite this, Ireland was renowned for producing children 'in their full strength with beautiful upright bodies and handsome well-complexioned faces'.

THE IMPORTANCE OF BAPTISM

It was an age when people believed quite fervently that if a baby were to be redeemed from original sin, it had to be baptised – and quickly. Most newborn babies were baptised within seven days of birth. A midwife could even baptise a dying baby before delivery was completed, simply by repeating the words: 'God's creature, I hereby baptise thee in the name of the Father, the Son and the Holy Ghost.' This was essential because church law demanded that an unbaptised baby be buried outside the churchyard.

Total immersion was still practised by some priests in rural districts as late as the 13th century but, from the 10th century onwards, there was a gradual move throughout Europe towards sprinkling the naked baby with water in the presence of its godparents. A pinch of salt was placed in the infant's mouth, and the chest and back rubbed with oil. Baptism was supposed to ensure a healthier life for a child physically and spiritually, curing illness or removing a congenital handicap. In remote parts of Europe, it was thought that baptism would protect a child from drowning or being eaten by wolves.

Births were occasions for an assertion of status. The choice of godparents could be equally important. It was usual to choose two of the baby's sex and one of the opposite sex. Although grandparents were not uncommon choices, many parents took this opportunity to extend ties of kinship or to create a connection with a powerful patron.

A DAY IN THE LIFE OF

A MEDIEVAL WET NURSE

A RELIABLE WET NURSE in a prosperous area could expect regular employment during the Middle Ages. Peasant families could not afford their services, but nobles and wealthy merchants sent for the wet nurse as soon as a baby was born. Indeed, most of our knowledge of how mothers behaved during this time comes from contemporary instructions to wet nurses.

A wet nurse would wake to feed the baby in her charge after a refreshing night's sleep. She would feed the baby and then eat breakfast herself, avoiding food that was 'salt, sharp, acid or styptic' – in particular, garlic. As well as feeding the child, a wet nurse was instructed to pick up children if they fell, nurse them if they cried, teach them to speak (by repeating words over and over again – so close that the nurse was to 'breathe on the child's tongue'), whisper and sing to them, stroke them when they slept, and bathe and anoint them.

When an infant was old enough to take solid food, a wet nurse might still be employed, to chew meat until the infant grew its own teeth. Early solid food in a well-to-do family might include pieces of chicken, pheasant or breast of partridge, 'the size and shape of an acorn'. An infant, it was said, 'can hold them in his hand and play with them, and sucking from them he will swallow some of it'.

MUM TO MANY A wet nurse with children in a 14th-century Italian hospital.

THE RITES OF BAPTISM A 15th-century baptismal font occupies pride of place at St Gregory's Church, Sudbury, Suffolk. A bishop presides at a baptism (top right) with parents and several godparents in attendance.

GROWING UP IN THE MIDDLE AGES

Childhood was a time for play, make-believe and dressing up.

But it did not last long. For boy or girl, rich or poor, the real business of life

began in earnest at the age of seven – at court, in school or on the land.

THE MOTHERS AND FATHERS of the Middle Ages generally took little interest in children under the age of five or so – perhaps because so many of them died before then. Beyond the age of six, however, there is evidence of greater bonding, and adults were even encouraged to play with their children. Nevertheless, discipline was often strict. According to Bartholomew the Englishman, the 13th-century encyclopedist, 'when he is especially loved by his father [a son] does not appear to be loved, because he is even more stricken by scoldings and beatings, lest he become insolent.' At the same time, the Italian Philip of Novara recommended a strict upbringing for children: 'few children perish from excess of severity, but many from being permitted too much.'

Peasant children were sometimes

AESOP'S FABLES A 15th-century French manuscript illustrates *The Wolf and the Lamb*, one of the many fables told to children.

given rough rag dolls to play with or balls made from scraps of cloth and leather, or even dead farmyard chicks, but toys were largely the playthings of the rich. Some were educational, such as the horn book – a piece of paper pasted onto a small oblong sheet of wood with a handle, and covered with a wafer thin, transparent sliver of horn. The piece of paper had the letters of the alphabet beautifully inscribed on it, and perhaps a prayer as well. Most medieval toys, however, were designed for fun rather than information.

In both castle and town house, girls and boys frequently played with rattles, quoits, skates, wheeled wooden carts, skipping ropes, kites, blocks, bones, balls, hoops, dolls, jumping-jacks, spinning-tops, seesaws, small windmills, little wooden boats, toy soldiers, whistles, clay birds, marionettes, glass rings, drums and cymbals.

YOUNG WARRIORS
A young would-be knight
tilts at a horseshoe.

BLOODY PURSUITS A taste for the popular sport of cock-fighting was acquired at a tender age in the Middle Ages.

CHILDREN AT PLAY Violence was a theme of many medieval recreations. Here, children watch a Punch and Judy show.

YOUNG PRETENDERS From an early age children played at being knights. Here, two boys fight with shields and clubs.

PIGGYBACK Fighting on piggyback was an early introduction to the adult pastime of mounted combat.

Cock-shy The bird was pelted until it collapsed. The first person to knock it over took it home to cook and eat.

Children loved to dress up as knights or ladies at court, for medieval games were generally games of imitation. Whereas peasant children played with shells, pretending they were sieves, and sticks, pretending they were ploughs and harrows, richer children had rocking horses, hobby horses and miniature bows and arrows to mimic the doughty warriors they had seen at tournaments.

As well as toys and nursery rhymes, children could choose from a range of games, many of which are still played today: marbles (originally played with nuts or small stones), top-whipping, stilt-walking, badminton, skipping, leapfrog, fives stones (jumping-jacks), ducks and drakes, bowling a hoop, Blindman's Buff (also called Hoodman Blind), see-saw (also called titter-totter), Hide and Seek (also called Hunt-the-Fox or Hunt-the-Hare), bobbing for apples or cherries and, finally, peek-a-boo.

Very few agricultural workers would have understood the concept of an animal as a pet. A peasant might keep a mongrel or two for hunting or for the protection of his cottage, and there were certainly working sheepdogs in England, Wales, Spain, France and Italy. But there was seldom enough food to go round for pets. For the wealthy, things were different. Castle pets included lap dogs, tame squirrels and mice, magpies, thrushes and robins, and possibly a cat or two to keep down vermin – though cats were still regarded by some as witches' 'familiars'. Working animals kept by the rich included hounds, falcons, hawks and horses. Those who had travelled far as Crusaders or pilgrims, kept more exotic pets – parrots, bears and even leopards.

The *Romance of Alexander*, an English illustrated manuscript of 1340, has pictures of cock-fighting and cock-throwing, for few people had scruples about cruelty to animals. Bull, bear and boar baiting were common all over Europe, and badgers suffered similarly, chained to a post in a small pit to be savaged by a pack of mastiffs, wolfhounds or other breeds of fighting dog.

Up to the age of six was reckoned to be the time of true childhood, of play and make-believe, of little work and often of very little education. Children were not expected to act as tiny adults; and medieval literature is scattered with reminiscences such as that of the 11th-century cleric Gerald of Wales who recalled how he and his brothers had played on the sands – his brothers building sandcastles while he built a sand-monastery.

Much of this happy-go-lucky approach changed abruptly at seven. What happened then depended on the child's class and gender. Peasant girls learnt to cook, weave and spin: boys to plough, reap, and tend animals. The sons of rich and ambitious parents, on the other hand, were sent to the local lord's castle or manor house to train as pages and then squires, or even to the Royal Court, which was described by the Englishman Sir John Fortescue in about

Bird Catching
A hunter nets a songbird; they were valued as pets.

1470 as 'the supreme academy for the nobles of the realm, and a school of vigour, probity and manners by which the realm is honoured and will flourish'. Such an education was designed to prepare the child for success in this world, rather than salvation in the next – as had been the case in the early Middle Ages when many seven-year-olds had been sent to monasteries.

Once in the service of a lord or noble, these boys would wear a uniform or livery. They trained in the martial arts and in horsemanship but also studied music and dancing. Strictest of all were lessons in manners and etiquette. 'Do not claw your head or your back,' one anonymous 15th-century authority told them, 'as if you were after a flea. Retch not, nor spit too far, nor laugh, nor speak too loud. Beware of making faces or scowling; and be no liar with your mouth. Do not lick your lips or drivel ... Do not lick a dish with your tongue to get at the dust.' The advice was sound, but it had to be repeated often; indeed, there were many nobles whose manners and behaviour were appalling.

THE YOUNG SQUIRE

A page was junior to a squire. His duties included assisting his lord to bathe and dress, looking after his lord's clothes, and waiting on him at table. In return he was taught by senior members of his lord's household how to ride, fight, hawk, play chess and backgammon, sing, dance and compose verses – all of which were essential components of the chivalric life.

When he reached his teens and became a squire, a youth was trained to fight with lance and sword, and learned the complicated rules of heraldry and jousting. The squire was expected to accompany his lord

PLAY SCHOOL A pupil pretends to be teacher. He is on the right, holding a palmer – a stick with a paddle at one end for smacking the hands of miscreants.

to war, leading his horse into battle and, in earlier medieval times, holding the reins when the fighting was on foot. It was a dangerous role, and many squires were killed or wounded in battle. Academic studies included the seven 'liberal arts': Grammar, Logic, Rhetoric, Arithmetic, Geometry, Astronomy and Music. The idea was that a true knight should be well educated, as well as a fine warrior.

Entry into formal knighthood came only after seven years' service as a squire, in a lengthy ritual of homage and dedication. The squire cleansed his body, donned white clothes and a red robe, and stood or knelt before the altar in the castle chapel for ten hours through the night, alone in silent prayer. At dawn, Mass was said, and the young knight was then presented to his lord by two sponsors. The lord handed the knight the sword and shield which had been placed on the altar during the vigil. An older knight then struck the young knight's neck or cheek with the flat of his hand or the side of his sword. This was the one blow the knight could never return. The young knight then swore a holy oath to dedicate his sword to good causes. The ceremony ended with a display of horsemanship, martial games and mock duels that lasted several days.

Like their brothers, many girls from noble families were sent to other households to finish their education in service. There, they would learn the elaborate manners necessary to hold a place in polite society and such accomplishments as music and dancing, riding, archery and, of course, needlework.

Parents, priests and the village community provided an entirely practical education for the sons and daughters of peasants, based largely on word of mouth or

first-hand experience. In *The Good Shepherd*, a French book of the 14th century written by Jean de Brie, a whole range of tasks for peasant children were graded according to age.

THE YOUNG PEASANT

Seven-year-old peasant boys and girls were to tend geese and to scare birds from the fields; eight-year-olds were to herd swine; nine-year-olds were to help with the ploughing and to look after small herds of cows; eleven-year-olds were expected to feed, clip, anoint, and guard flocks of sheep. (Giotto, later to become one of the great artists heralding the Italian Renaissance, was tending a flock of sheep at that age.) By the time they reached 14, boys and girls were fully fledged shepherds, ready to look after 300 or more sheep. Children were given plenty of other work to do – feeding horses, drawing water, weeding, removing stones from the fields, pick-

JUSTICE
An English farmer waits to catch a young fruit thief.

ing vegetables, binding sheaves of corn, sowing seed, threshing, thatching, cutting peat for fuel, and gathering firewood. Girls did all or any of these tasks, and were also expected to mind their younger brothers and sisters, to help with the cooking, and to gather wild fruit and berries.

EDUCATION IN THE TOWNS

At 14, the son of a skilled craftsman was apprenticed to a master. His father signed the articles of apprenticeship which bound the young boy to seven years' hard work, learning his trade. The apprentice had to produce his 'master-piece', to show that he had learned his craft before he moved on to work as journeyman for another master, eventually earning membership of the local Guild of Master Craftsmen.

During the Middle Ages, more and more children in towns had access to education. It became fashionable for a wealthy merchant to bequeath money for the foundation of a school or college in town. The curriculum varied very little from country to country and was taught in Latin. The main emphasis for boys was on Latin grammar and texts (hence, 'grammar schools'), philosophy and some French, even if it was their native language; they also studied music, dance and riding. At Eton College, which was founded by Henry VI of England, scholars began their working day at 5am; it lasted, with breaks for meals and divine

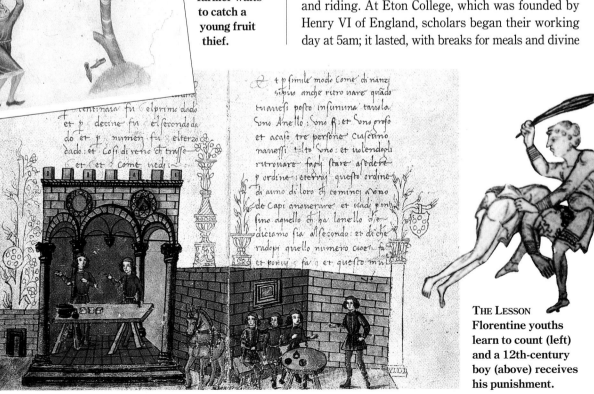

THE LESSON
Florentine youths learn to count (left) and a 12th-century boy (above) receives his punishment.

וּבַהֲמֹיֹה וּבִישָׂרֵיהּ אֲחוֹשָׁרֵיהּ לֹא יִגְבֵּר וְלֹא יִגְאַל כָּל חֵרֶם קֹדֶשׁ קָדָשִׁים הוּא לַיהוָה כָּל חֵרֶם אֲשֶׁר
יָחֳרַם מִן הָאָדָם לֹא יִפָּדֶה מוֹת יוּמַת וְכֹל בִּעְשַׂר הָאָרֶץ מִזֶּרַע הָאָרֶץ וּמִפְּרֵי הָעֵץ לַיהוָה
הוּא קֹדֶשׁ לַיהוָה וְאִם גָּאַל יִגְאַל אִישׁ מִמַּעֲשֵׂרוֹ חֲמִישִׁתוֹ יֹסֵף עָלָיו וְכָל מַעֲשַׂר בָּקָר
וָצֹאן כָּל אֲשֶׁר יַעֲבֹר תַּחַת הַשָּׁבֶט הָעֲשִׂירִי יִהְיֶה קֹּדֶשׁ לַיהוָה לֹא יְבַקֵּר בֵּין טוֹב לָרַע וְלֹא
יְמִירֶנּוּ וְאִם הָמֵר יְמִירֶנּוּ וְהָיָה הוּא וּתְמוּרָתוֹ יִהְיֶה קֹדֶשׁ לֹא יִגָּאֵל אֵלֶּה הַמִּצְוֹת אֲשֶׁר
צִוָּה יְהוָה אֶת מֹשֶׁה אֶל בְּנֵי יִשְׂרָאֵל בְּהַר סִינָי ׃

חֲזַק

סִימָן סְכוּם פְּסוּקֵי רְסִמְדָּא נָטַ״ל

MASTER AND PUPIL   A Hebrew manuscript of the late 15th century shows the interior of a Jewish school.

TELLING THE TIME

For centuries, unreliable 'clocks' had been used. Then

clockmakers in Europe gradually invented ways to master time.

IN THE MIDDLE AGES, most 'clocks' relied on gravity to drive them – the controlled flow of water along channels, or grains slipping from the top to the bottom of a sand glass. Alternatively, people marked candles or glass vessels of oil, with the amount of tallow or oil burnt indicating how many hours had passed. Or they used the sundial, which was already some 2500 years old by the 11th century. But none of these methods was reliable. Candles burnt at irregular speeds, according to the quality of the tallow used. Water clocks were cumbersome; it was almost impossible to regulate a

constant flow of water through them, and they were susceptible to freezing in winter. The sand glass was the most accurate way of measuring the passing of an hour or two, but it needed repeated turning 24 hours a day if it was to be used as a clock.

The problem of telling the time was even more fundamental than this, however. Until the invention of the mechanical clock, the day in most of Europe was divided into two periods – daylight and darkness – each of which was reckoned to last 12 hours, whatever the time of year. Therefore, in winter, when the period of daylight was shorter, an English daylight hour lasted only 38 minutes (in modern time), whereas in summer, when daylight lasted longer, an hour was twice as long. Without some clockwork mechanism, it was impossible to divide the day and night into hours of equal length and show at a glance what the time was at any given moment. Most early mechanical clocks that existed were not used to tell the time: they were astronomical clocks, used instead to forecast the movements of the sun, the moon and the five known planets.

The first breakthrough was the development of a weight-driven mechanical clock for telling the time. This came in the early 13th century, when a Frenchman, Villard de Honnecourt, invented a machine driven by clockwork that rotated the statue of an angel on the east face of Chartres Cathedral. In 1271 a clockmaker named

SET IN STONE **Carved stone sundials mounted on the walls of buildings were the forerunners of church clocks.**

Robert the Englishman complained that he and his fellows were still unable to perfect their work as they could not yet 'make a disc of uniform weight in every part'.

Five years later, a clockmaker at the court of King Alphonso X of Castile invented an improved mechanism for driving a clock. For the disc, he substituted a revolving drum that leaked mercury at a constant rate: far less mercury was needed than water to drive such a clock; mercury did not freeze, and it was easier to regulate the flow. By the end of the 13th century, clocks had been installed in many cathedrals, and in 1300 the first public clock was displayed in Paris.

But it was not until the middle of the 14th century that clockmaking

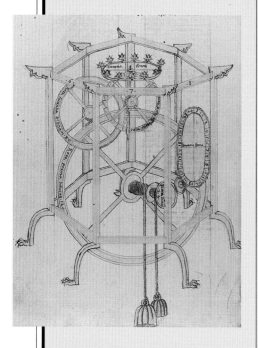

CLOCKWORK **A contemporary drawing of Giovanni di Dondi's astronomical clock, made at Padua in northern Italy and completed in 1364.**

TRAVELLING CLOCK
A 10th-century portable sundial – an ancient but not entirely reliable way of telling the time.

FANTASY TIME A fanciful, late 15th-century clock. Right: An astronomical clock in St Mark's Square, Venice.

ALARM CALL An example of a 14th-century mechanical chiming clock. The weights operate a crank that shakes the bell, which has a stone inside it, causing it to rattle on each hour.

advanced beyond this stage. Over 16 years, the Italian Giovanni di Dondi built a clock that later became famous throughout Europe. Giovanni di Dondi's clock had many astronomical functions, but it included as well a 24-hour dial, starting at noon and revolving counter-clockwise, with a fixed point alongside the dial indicating the time.

Within a few years mechanical clocks appeared in most great Italian cities and then all over Europe. The first clock to strike equal hours was on the Church of St Gothard in Milan, 'a wonderful clock,' reported a contemporary chronicler, 'which at the first hour of the night gives one sound, at the second two strikes . . . and so distinguishes one hour from another, which is of greatest use to men of every degree'. With a similar aim in mind, Charles V of France decreed that churches throughout his kingdom were to ring their bells at hourly intervals.

A split developed between East and West in Europe. The Orthodox Church in the East refused to use clocks or to mark the passing of the hours, viewing such practices as a challenge to the concept of eternity. The Roman Catholic Church in the West, on the other hand, embraced the new technology. The concept of time measured by clocks had arrived.

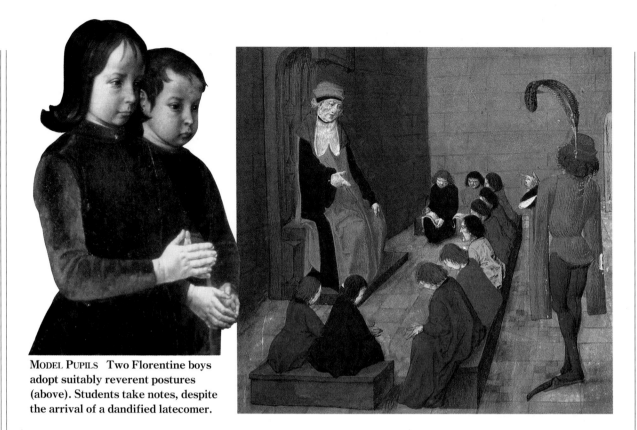

MODEL PUPILS Two Florentine boys adopt suitably reverent postures (above). Students take notes, despite the arrival of a dandified latecomer.

service, until 5pm. Learning and discipline were enforced through the birch – 'The birch twigs are so sharp, It maketh me have a faint heart,' wrote one schoolboy poet.

Girls, on the other hand, learnt to speak French (the language spoken by most educated people in Europe), to curtsy, embroider, preserve fruit, to play musical instruments, and to dance and sing. Most schools attempted to teach children to read, though books were scarce before the invention of printing.

There were no school uniforms, but rules in most countries placed restrictions on what children should wear. These centred round people's social standing and, since medieval governments were anxious to preserve the status quo, often applied to adults as well as children. The wives and children of tradesmen were to wear: 'No veils, but such as are made with thread, nor any kinds of furs, excepting those of lambs, rabbits, cats or foxes.' A 14th-century act of the English Parliament also decreed that 'all labourers and lower classes of people shall wear no kind of cloth but blankets and russets, nor use any girdles than such as are made of linen.'

Schools became steadily harsher as the Middle Ages progressed. As early as the 8th century, an English Benedictine monk ran a monastic school where children were comfortably dressed, adequately fed and warmly housed in winter. They were also given periods of recreation each day, and they were even rewarded for good behaviour with gifts of sweets; nor was there any corporal punishment. Some 500 years later, however, at the cathedral school in Chartres in central France, each student had to learn a poem or story every day and recite it, to make sure the memory of it was not 'precipitated to flight'. Failure to remember it resulted in a harsh beating. In the 12th century, Guibert, later Abbot of Nogent in France, was showered with blows on many occasions by a tutor whom he considered incompetent.

What changed steadily over the years was the Church's view of children. To St Anselm, the Italian monk and Archbishop of Canterbury writing in about 1100, children were weak souls who needed 'gentleness from others, kindness, compassion, cheerful encouragement, loving forbearance ...' But to later clerics, children were creatures of sin whose spirits had to be broken lest the devil take possession of them. 'Take a smart rod and beat them' was the advice given to parents of disobedient children by the French author of *The Knight of the Tour Landry*. The book was translated into English, printed by Caxton in the 15th century, and its advice widely followed.

LIFE IN THE MEDIEVAL HOME

Few people could relax at home. Medieval dwellings lacked air, light,
comfort and, above all, privacy. Home was a public place – the well-to-do shared
their houses with servants, clerks and retainers; the poor shared their huts and
hovels with pigs, cows and chickens. Even kings endured discomfort –
at Westminster Palace in London the garbage from the royal kitchen was
carried through the king's halls. It made the courtiers sick.

FROM CASTLE TO COTTAGE

Noble households included vast retinues of chamberlains, stewards, bailiffs, knights,

squires and assorted men-at-arms. Nobles and city merchants alike enjoyed flaunting their

power and wealth. Serfs' cottages, meanwhile, were bare in the extreme.

 HROUGHOUT THE MIDDLE AGES, the building materials most frequently used were those found nearest to hand: timber where there were forests, or stone where there were quarries. By the 15th century, however, bricks were being made in many parts of Europe, particularly in Flanders. Roofs were of tile, slate, thatch, turf, timber or lead. Some homes were strong enough to withstand sieges and the pounding of early cannon: others were so fragile that a neighbour with a grudge could demolish them single-handed.

All types of medieval dwelling – the castle, the town house and the cottage – had something in common. They were dark, cold, damp, and reeked of smoke. Only in mutual discomfort, and a complete lack of privacy, were the social strata of the Middle Ages united. Married couples would sleep in the same room as their servants or children; and the kings of England even had a senior official, the 'groom of the stool', to wipe the royal bottom.

Nobles built castles as homes, as defences, as prisons for their enemies, and as strongholds from which they could subdue the surrounding countryside. Attack was often the best means of defence – and there was much to menace a medieval baron. There was the threat of 'disseisin' by king or emperor, whereby a baron could be evicted from his castle by force – always quicker and more effective than resorting to the law. There was the fear of armed insurrection. And there was the threat of foray – a raid by a rival baron, freebooters or foreign troops.

Even in the 15th century, many gentlemen's houses continued to be constructed with defence in mind. Although they could not resist siege engines or guns, their moats, ramparts and massive gate towers with drawbridges were reasonably effective against

A DAY IN THE LIFE OF

A STEWARD IN THE 11TH CENTURY

ACCORDING TO THE INSTRUCTIONS laid down for a steward in one anonymous 11th-century manuscript, 'the seneschal [steward] of lands ought to be prudent and faithful and profitable, and he ought to know the law of the realm to protect his lord's business.'

On large estates two stewards were often appointed: one to look after the domestic management of the household, the other to look after the baronial domain.

The steward was a busy man. He rose early and attended his lord in the Great Hall, showing him the estate accounts and presenting any problems or disputes that had broken out among the tenants. In the afternoon, he rode around the estate, examining timber, crops, harvests, and seed supplies. At least three times a year, he was expected to visit all the manors on the lord's estate, checking rents, services, customs and dues.

'He ought to know how many acres there are in each field ... if the provost account for more seed than is right, and thereby he can see how many ploughs are required on the manor ... and further he can see how many acres ought to be reaped ... and if there be any cheating in the sowing, or ploughing, or reaping ... and how much hay is necessary every year for the sustenance of the manor ... and how much stock can be kept.'

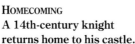

**HOMECOMING
A 14th-century knight
returns home to his castle.**

BRIDAL FEAST The Burgundian noblewoman Clarisse de Montauban presides at a banquet while musicians play and pheasant is served to lords and ladies.

assault. Nevertheless, the size of the new windows, the elaborate external decoration and the increasing use of brick rather than stone indicate that both the fortified manor-house and the combined home and fortress that was the medieval castle were giving way to the country house.

A LICENCE TO BUILD

Since the loyalties of subjects could change overnight, kings reserved the right to refuse permission to build or reinforce a castle. Anyone who built a castle in defiance of the king's command had to make sure that he had the strength to prevent its forcible seizure and demolition by the king. Licences to build were granted informally, and verbal rather than written permission was usually enough.

But the licensing system often failed, because the need to build strongholds and places of safety was greatest when law and order broke down. When Charlemagne's great empire in western Europe was divided by his heirs in the 9th century, many barons took the opportunity to build castles, initially for self-protection but subsequently to preserve their own independence from the king.

Castles were busy places, employing large numbers of people, proportionate to the social status of the owner. At the top, the Royal Household was the nerve-centre of national politics and administration. Households of great lords mirrored on a smaller scale that of the king, and the semi-official Black Book of the [English] Royal Household of 1472 listed models of households for different ranks: a duke's might total 240 people, including four knights and 40 esquires and gentlemen, while an ordinary knight might have 16.

After the lord, his lady and their immediate family, the most important member of the household was the chamberlain. It was his job to make sure that the Great Hall and Chamber of the castle were adequately supplied and to attend to the lord of the manor. Next in importance was the steward or seneschal, the overseer of all his lord's domain who granted leases on land or property, planned the manor's economy and kept the castle supplied. The chancellor's main duties were to say Mass (in the castle chancel – hence his name), to offer prayers and grace before meals, and to attend to his lord's personal and official correspondence. The bailiff saw to the day-to-day running of the estate: ploughing, marling (ensuring the fields were kept fertile), mowing and sowing fields; repairing fences; and looking after the estate

cattle. Other resident domestic staff included smiths, carpenters, farriers, armourers, ushers, cooks, a pantler and a butler, a butcher, a baker and, indeed, a candlestick maker.

A great castle was also home to a large number of knights and men-at-arms, squires, watchmen, archers, crossbowmen, and sub-tenants who acted as sentries on the battlements at times of danger. Their numbers varied according to the size of the castle, but often a large castle had its own small army. Krak des Chevaliers, the awe-inspiring Crusader castle in Syria, had a garrison of over 2000 men in 1212.

A visitor to Sir John Fastolf's castle at Caister in Norfolk in the 1450s would have been dazzled by the gold ewers, silver platters, and the gilt gallon-pots enamelled with Fastolf's arms. If the visitor had penetrated into Fastolf's chamber, he would have admired the bed-hangings of areas around the feather bed and the 'six white cushions'. But the visitor would

TOWERS OF THE MIGHTY The Duc de Berry's castle at Saumur in the 14th century was both home and fortress.

LIGHTING IN THE MIDDLE AGES

THE CHEAPEST FORM OF LIGHTING was the rush dip, a taper made from the stalks of rushes, which were dried in the sun, peeled down one side (leaving a strip to keep the rush reasonably stiff), cut into lengths of about a foot, and then dipped into hot melted fat, preferably lard. The spongy inside of the rush soaked up the fat. After each dipping, the rush was left to dry until it looked like a modern taper. It was then placed in a small receptacle called a 'nip', where it provided a weak light for about half an hour.

Candles were also home-made, from animal fat. They lasted longer and gave a much better light. They were usually placed in candlesticks of wood, iron or more precious metals. Although the light of torches was not cast as evenly as that of candles, it was still common in the later Middle Ages to use them – often held by servants – to light a large space such as the Great Hall of a castle. When King Jean II of France died in captivity in London in 1364, Edward III provided 4000 torches (each of them

FLICKERING LIGHT Firelight and a candle illuminate this household scene. Left: two candlesticks and 14th-century lanterns.

12 feet high) and 3000 candles (each weighing 10 pounds) to light the dead King's funeral service.

Lanterns (or 'lanthorns'), meanwhile, were simple: a candle was stuck into a metal frame with very thin sides of transparent horn.

have been less impressed by the furniture, of which little was mentioned in the inventory except two chairs in the Hall and a folding-table and two chairs in Fastolf's chamber. With the exception of beds – which people often used as chairs – household furniture was still fairly limited.

THE CASTLE DAY

The entire household rose at cockcrow. The lord and lady attended Mass, either in the private chapel or at a portable altar in the Great Hall. The first meal of the day was a piece of bread and a cup of ale, with

perhaps a slice of cold meat. After this, the lord and his seneschal met to discuss business and administrative matters in the Hall. A succession of tenants attended, with complaints, disputes relating to the inheritance of land on the castle estates, and requests for permission to marry.

By mid-morning, the lord and his staff would be hungry, and the main meal of the day was served at trestle tables in the Hall. The lord and lady dined off silverware, while others ate off horn, earthenware or wooden vessels. Since kitchens were well away from living quarters, and since the Hall was generally on

A MEDIEVAL CASTLE

THE MEDIEVAL CASTLE was more than a military base. It was also a home and storehouse, a place for living, feasting and recreation. Many castles were protected by a moat, others were built high on pinnacles of rock, in either case to hinder would-be attackers. The most fortified part of a castle was the towered keep, usually built at the heart of its system of defences.

Here were the stables, armoury, guardhouse and storerooms. On the first floor were the living quarters for the officers and men of the garrison, with more storerooms for food and grain, including feed for the horses and other livestock. Below ground level, at the base of one of the towers, was the castle dungeon.

Crenellated battlements topped the walls that ran along the sides of the castle. On one side were the servants' kitchen and hall, with their sleeping quarters above and, on the other side, the lord and lady's apartments – the bedchamber and grandchamber. Below these rooms was the castle chapel.

To the rear of the castle was its largest and most imposing room – the Great Hall – with its high table on a dais for the lord and lady and their important guests, and trestle tables for the castle stewards and officers. Overlooking the Great Hall was the minstrels' gallery. Leading from the Hall was the buttery, where food was prepared for serving at table, and the kitchen where it was cooked. Below these rooms were the wine cellars.

Most castles had their own wells, often in the central courtyard, and their own latrines, in one of the towers abutting the Great Hall.

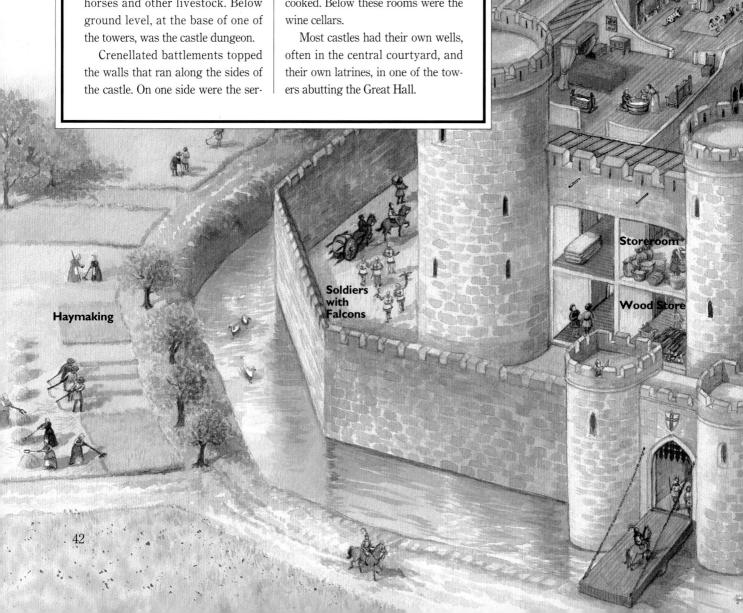

Great Chamber

Storeroom

Wood Store

Soldiers with Falcons

Haymaking

Latrine

Great Hall

Minstrels' Gallery

Kitchen

Buttery

Servants' Hall

Kitchen Garden

Guardroom

Armoury

Dungeon

43

the first or second floor of the castle, the food was usually served cold. At the end of the meal, the almoner collected scraps of meat and bread for distribution among the poor who waited at the gate.

In the afternoon, the lord went hunting or hawking, while his lady stayed in the castle to embroider fine cloth, or perhaps to gossip with her female attendants. The women told each other tales and riddles, and were joined by the children once lessons with the tutor were finished.

Most evenings the lord took a bath on his return from hunting, sitting on a stool in a wooden tub of warm water in his bedchamber. The soap was a strong-smelling substance made of animal fat, wood ash and soda. Having dressed in fine clothes, the lord presided over supper in the Hall. This was less substantial than dinner, but it was accompanied by music and other entertainment. Once the lord retired for the night, the captain of the guard posted sentries … and so the castle went to bed.

THE TOWN HOUSE

Medieval town houses were noisy, smelly and crowded. A three-storey building often housed ten or more families, each in a single room. Many towns-people still kept animals, and the streets were choked with reeking piles of excrement, the entrails and blood of slaughtered animals, rotting vegetables and heaps of manure. Every town of any size paid workers to remove the rubbish that accumulated, but the streets remained covered with filth. Privies ran into open drains or leaking cesspits. Water supplies were polluted, and the air was filled with smoke.

By the 15th century, London was five or six times bigger than any other English town. When people spoke of London, they meant a straggle of great houses, streets, buildings and communities which stretched from the Royal Household at Westminster, beside the shops and taverns of the City, past the Tower to the baths and brothels of Southwark. It was a crowded city, where large merchant houses, often with business premises attached, rubbed shoulders with the hovels of the poor.

The city merchant wanted three things from his house: comfort, a showcase for his wealth and possessions, and protection from thieves and marauders. Merchants' houses were decorated with rich tapestries and murals, but furniture was rough-and-ready – serviceable rather than beautiful. Windows of town houses were larger than those in castles and, by the 15th century, glass was beginning to replace the oiled cloth that had previously hung in windows. Doors were usually strong, of thick wood, and all windows were shuttered.

EYEWITNESS

A HOUSEWIFE WRITES ABOUT HOUSEHOLD CHORES

THE SURVIVAL OF LETTERS written by three generations of the Paston family throughout the 15th century gives us a series of illuminating first-hand accounts of everyday life at that time. The Pastons were a wealthy family living in Norfolk, a prosperous sheep-raising region in England. Here is Margaret Paston writing to her husband about some building work, possibly on their town house in Norwich.

❝ I have taken the measure in the drawing chamber, where you want your coffers and desk to be set for a while; and there is no space beside the bed, even though the bed were removed to the door, to set both your board [writing-table] and your coffers and to have space to go and sit beside it. Wherefore I have arranged that you shall have the same drawing chamber as you had before, where you shall lie by yourself; and when your gear is removed out of your little house, the door shall be locked and your bags laid in one of the great coffers, so that they shall be safe, I trust. ❞

KEEPING COUNT A wealthy lady compiles a household inventory.

Ay intention de
parler des char
dmes et de sart
de leur labourai
ge et de toutes les herbes
qui y font semees pour no
reture de corps humain Et
auec ceulx par le diray en
semble De celles qui sans
labourer viennent ailleurs
par leur nature et vertu du
soleil est en suay par lor
& e selon le latin
ay aussi la vertu

qui puet aidier et nuyre au
corps Car ce vault par espe
cial au corps de ceulx qui
demeurent aup champs qui
ne pruent auoir mediance
composees a leurs plaisirs
Cy parle des vertus des her
bes en commun ..

Tous disons que larbre
seulement contient
la parfaute nature de la
plante et en larbre les
proprietez des elementaires
festomgnent plus des excellen

HOMES AND GARDENS Gardeners work in a walled garden (above). The houses and their gardens that lined 15th-century streets (left) were grander than ever before.

As the 14th century progressed, chairs became less of a luxury and gradually replaced the wooden benches. The trestle table was still common, but wealthier citizens were beginning to favour solid, free-standing tables of oak or sycamore, covered with a linen cloth. In addition, most rooms had one or more wooden chests, for storing salt, clothes, linen, tools and even armour. Food was stored in small cupboards with perforated

45

A Florentine Palazzo

A RICH MERCHANT'S HOUSE served two purposes: it provided comfortable living accommodation for his family, and also – in the opulence of its architecture and fittings – gave him the opportunity to display his wealth and status.

At ground level, the house had few windows, and such as it had were small and barred. Indeed, the crenellated walls that surrounded the garden and the massive doors giving on to the street made the palazzo look as much like a castle as a house. Most householders in towns and cities lived in constant fear of thieves and housebreakers.

People sat on stone seats outside the front door as they waited to be let in. The main door led from the bustle of the street with its shops selling wine and cloth into a large courtyard with cloistered passages to the sides. Off these passages were the ground-floor kitchen and storerooms. There was also a basement room where people would rest in summer to escape the heat.

On the first floor – or *pianonobile* as it was known in Florentine houses – were some of the bedrooms and also the lavish assembly room where the merchant would formally receive his guests and entertain them to dinner.

On the second floor of the palazzo were more bedrooms, the merchant's study and the principal bedchamber, in the later Middle Ages complete with four-poster bed. Rods were suspended outside the windows for drying clothes. Above, on the top floor, were more storerooms – for apples, raisins, olives and so on – and laundry rooms.

Storeroom

Loggia

Wine Shop

dy

Pianonobile

Kitchen

Basement

47

doors. Beds were simple affairs, consisting of wooden frames with holes, through which ropes were knotted in a crisscross pattern to form a base. On this would rest a straw-filled mattress and blankets of rough wool. People covered the floors with herbs and grasses in the summer, and with rushes and straw in the winter, which became infested with fleas or soiled by animal droppings and grease. Or they might make life pleasanter for dinner guests by scattering violets and other flowers on the floor.

THE STRUCTURE OF A VILLAGE HOUSE

While barons and merchants flaunted their wealth and power, villagers in the Middle Ages built houses for one reason alone – to provide shelter for themselves and their animals. Throughout Europe, from Scandinavia to Italy, Spain to Hungary, the village house was much the same: a single-storey, wood-framed structure, with walls made of mixed clay, straw, cow manure and pebbles. Such houses were too flimsy to last for more than a generation or two, and were generally too small for the needs of the whole family. Within such draughty, leaking hovels four or five people lived in considerable discomfort.

Many cottages were built on a frame of timber crutches or 'crucks' – substantial curved beams sawn as one piece from the trunk of a large tree. Pairs of such beams were set opposite each other to form a series of arches along the length of the cottage. The open spaces between these arches were then filled with wattle and daub. Wattle, strands of willow usually made more flexible by soaking in water, was woven together to form panels which were then plastered with 'daub' – wet clay and straw, and a little cow dung to act as glue. Inside the cottage, a hanging curtain of rough cloth divided the dwelling into two chambers.

Windows were unglaz-

WINTER WARMER
Village women warm themselves in 15th-century France.

ed, and were probably little more than holes in the roof or gable-end, covered with cloth and wooden shutters. Cottages had no fireplace and no chimney, simply an open fire on the floor. The interior was, therefore, dark and smoky.

The floor consisted of bare earth, which the cottagers often scooped out to give themselves more headroom. The earth taken from the floor was then piled at the base of the crutches, to strengthen the frame of the house.

The hall served as a kitchen and storeroom. In times of plenty, smoked and salted food was stored on rafters, out of the reach of children and animals, of which there were many in most cottages. In 1201 a Cornish serf and his family kept two oxen, one cow, one mare, two pigs, nine sheep and eleven goats in their tiny cottage. Others used the cottage to store the crops that they grew on their strips of land.

Larger village houses were built on two floors, but even in these houses, peasants preferred to sleep with their livestock on the ground floor – to prevent them being stolen, and to keep warm. Giving evidence to the bishop's tribunal in Montaillou in France in the early 14th century, Raymonde Michel described the house of her father Pierre: 'In the cellar of our house there were two beds, one where my mother and father slept and the other for any heretic passing through [the word 'heretic' was bandied about a good deal, due to conflicts between the Cathar sect and the Catholic Church]. The cellar was next to the kitchen and had a door leading into it. No one slept on the floor above the cellar. My brothers and I slept in a room on the other side of the kitchen, so that the kitchen was between the children's room and the cellar where our parents slept. The cellar had an outside door opening on to the threshing floor.' Many houses grew in this way, with a room or even a whole storey being added as the need arose and money permitted.

Cottagers had few possessions. Apart from the rough curtain that hung behind the door, there was little cloth for other purposes. In many families there was only one bed. Most cottages had a homemade trestle table and a couple of benches, a chest and a cupboard. For cooking there were iron cauldrons and a few tin pans. Earthenware pots, crocks, bowls and jugs were used for storing and serving food. Farm tools hung on the walls of the cottage and perhaps a few baskets, a wooden bucket and a bathtub.

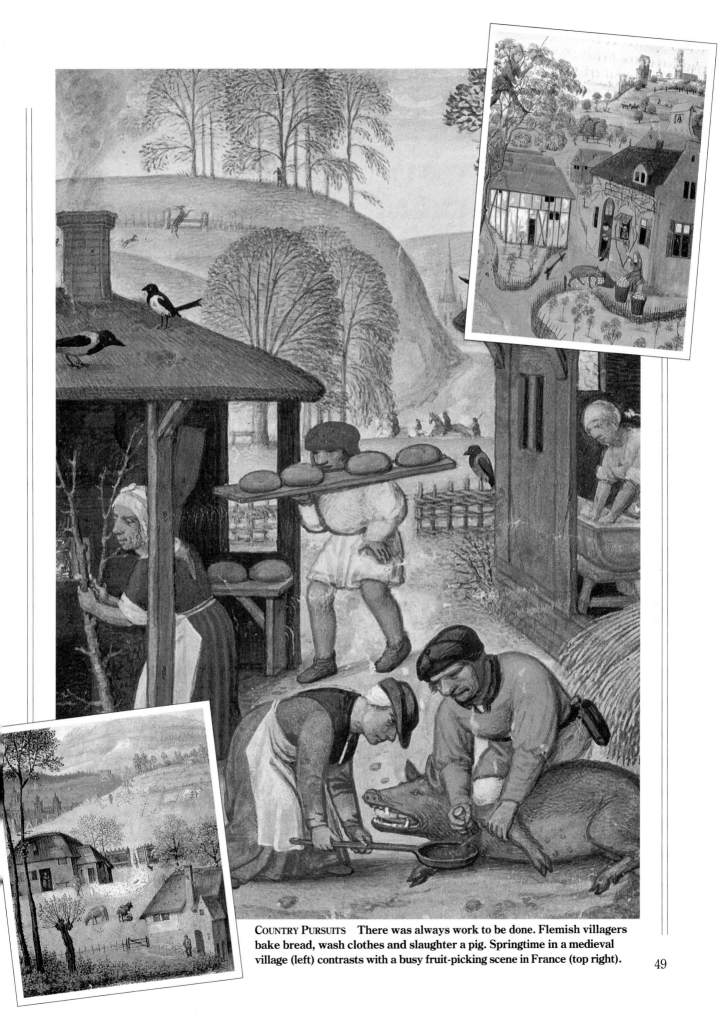

COUNTRY PURSUITS   There was always work to be done. Flemish villagers bake bread, wash clothes and slaughter a pig. Springtime in a medieval village (left) contrasts with a busy fruit-picking scene in France (top right).   49

VAULTS OF GLORY

From the solid Romanesque to the soaring Gothic, architectural

styles celebrated the confidence of man and the glory of God.

EUROPEAN BUILDINGS reflected changing times and a changing vision during the Middle Ages. Before the 11th century, buildings such as churches tended to be squat and solid. In the 11th century, however, increasing wealth in many European communities and a growing mastery of building techniques led to the emergence of the more sophisticated

Romanesque style, characterised by the round arch, whose height was determined by the radius of the distance it spanned.

The greatest builders of the Romanesque period, which reached its peak between 1075 and 1125, produced magnificent work. In England, this included the Great Hall of William Rufus at Westminster and the cathedral at Durham. Exceptional specimens in France included the immense abbey at Cluny, and in Germany the huge cathedrals at Trier, Mainz and Minden.

At the end of the 11th century, a new style of architecture began to appear, first in France, but quickly spreading to the Holy Roman Empire, Spain, England and the Low Countries. Gothic, as the style became known, was characterised by a better understanding of the stresses of buildings: the pointed arch enabled builders to gain far greater height,

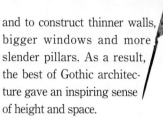

MEMORIAL Hans von Burghausen, the German architect, who died in 1432. Below: A pair of medieval masons' dividers.

and to construct thinner walls, bigger windows and more slender pillars. As a result, the best of Gothic architecture gave an inspiring sense of height and space.

With the new style came a new master craftsman – the architect-engineer – who designed the great buildings of medieval times and supervised their construction. These men were head-hunted by princes, archbishops and emperors.

Great competition existed both between cities and between builders. Not all spires were raised solely to the glory of God – the vanity of man also acted as a spur. There was intense professional rivalry to see

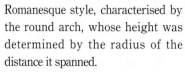

GOTHIC VAULTING The nave of Cologne Cathedral soars upwards, supported on slim pillars. Intricate systems of flying buttresses were built on the outsides of buildings, as at Chartres (left), to support the outward thrust created by the vaulting.

ROUND OR POINTED The nave of Durham Cathedral, with broad, solid pillars supporting rounded arches, is a fine example of the Romanesque style. Left: In the Gothic-style Bourges Cathedral in France, by contrast, the sense of height and space in the nave and side aisles is increased by the use of slim vaulting shafts that run from floor to ceiling.

who could build the highest vault, the most graceful arch, the loftiest spire, the most delicate tracery, the boldest flying buttress. Sometimes ambition outweighed technique. In 1284 the vault of the choir of Beauvais Cathedral came crashing down: it had been 156 feet high, equivalent to a 14-storey modern high-rise block. The spire of Strasbourg Cathedral stood safely, however, at a height of 466 feet, then the tallest building in the world. In Spain there were great Gothic cathedrals in Burgos, Toledo and Salamanca; it took over 100 years to build Seville Cathedral.

Hard to imagine today, looking at the sombre stonework inside a medieval cathedral, is that much of it would have been painted in green, red and white. Pigments such as vermilion or azurite (a deep blue) would have picked out the clothes and features of the carved figures.

There were also many great secular buildings – such as the warehouses at Lüneberg, the Hôtel Dieu at Beaune, the town halls at Louvain, Brussels, Brunswick and Barcelona, and the Schoner Brunnen fountain in Nuremberg.

ITALIAN ROMANESQUE
The façade of Pisa Cathedral is decorated with rows of small pillars and rounded arches, typical of the Romanesque style in Italy.

EATING AND DRINKING

For the poor, the staple diet was dark bread, curds, weak ale and boiled beans –

for the rich, roast meats, sugared fruits, good wine and dishes flavoured with Eastern spices.

But, for all, a poor harvest meant an empty stomach.

BY THE END OF the Middle Ages people were eating more and better food than at the beginning. Before 1300, all parts of Europe were heavily dependent on grain, and a crop failure in any year spelt famine and economic disaster. From 1350, however, food supplies became more readily available; and by 1450 a labourer could buy twice as much food as his ancestors 100 years before.

Improvements and changes in farming techniques during the early Middle Ages had allowed an ever-increasing population to be fed. The mouldboard plough not only cut through the soil but also turned it over, thus increasing agricultural efficiency. The introduction of the three-field system in which crops were rotated each year invigorated the soil and produced greater yields: wheat or rye grew in one field; legumes (beans, peas and lentils) in another; while the third was left fallow to rest.

Monks pioneered vegetable and fruit-growing and the use of herbs for medicinal and culinary purposes. Better roads meant food arrived fresher at market. And the Black Death of 1348 resulted in a far smaller population, so more food was available after 1348, and even the poor began to eat meat regularly. In the mid-14th century, the 90,000 citizens of Florence consumed 4000 oxen and calves, 60,000 sheep, 20,000 goats and 30,000 pigs in a single year – more than an animal each per head. In the 14th century, it was estimated

that there were over ten million sheep in England alone (with a population of three million people), producing 35 million gallons of milk and 35 million pounds of cheese.

THE RICH MAN'S TABLE

In the early Middle Ages, however, meat had been a sign of wealth. For display as much as anything else, the typical rich man's table would include a handsome array of beef, mutton, pork, poultry, venison, pigeon, goat, lamb, wild boar, rabbit, and a variety of freshwater fish.

Since it was not economic to feed livestock through the winter, the animals were generally slaughtered in the late autumn and their meat preserved in salt for the next six months. It took about two-pence worth of salt (2 pounds) to cure five-pence worth of meat (20 pounds). Noble households could afford the best dry salt, and employed a servant – the powderer – to break up rocks of salt for the kitchen. The next problem was how to take the taste of the salt away. From the 12th century onwards, the Crusaders brought back from the Middle East a liking for spices such as cinnamon, saffron, sugar, cardamom, cloves and pepper; and these became very popular. As accompaniments to meat, they also served sauces thickened with egg yolks, breadcrumbs or ground almonds.

The rich ate few vegetables and little raw fruit; lentils and cucumbers were regarded as particularly

FEASTING A French diner enjoys a cup of wine.

TRENCHERMEN At a banquet, servants bring new trenchers of bread to the table. A peasant (right) stacks sheaves of corn from the harvest.

unwholesome. 'Beware of salads, green foods and raw fruits' was a typical warning. Apples, cherries, pears, plums and other indigenous fruits were either preserved in honey or cooked in pies and pastries. As a result, their diet lacked fibre, and constipation was a major problem. The diet for all classes also lacked vitamin C, and diseases such as rickets and scurvy were widespread. So too were skin diseases – such as Chaucer's Summoner's 'whelks white … and

knobs sitting on his cheek' – and, given the state of medieval sanitation, food poisoning.

At a time when the climate was milder in northern Europe than it is today, many areas produced their own wine. There were vineyards in England as far north as Lincolnshire and Yorkshire, but most wine was imported from the English-held territories in south-west France. Wine was sometimes flavoured with ginger or cinnamon; and spicy mulled wine was

LOAVES AND FISHES
An Italian fish shop (right) does brisk trade around 1385.

HOT AND CRUSTY A baker (far left) uses a paddle to scoop bread from the oven. A baker is dragged through the street for selling underweight loaves.

popular in winter. Even the rich and young drank ale for breakfast, and water was rightly regarded with suspicion: it was generally contaminated, particularly in the towns where refuse often washed into the wells.

One of the best-known medieval cookbooks was the *Viandier de Taillevent*, written by the chief cook to King Charles V of France in 1373. The recipes were elaborate and ornate: stuffed pigs, herons and swans; peacocks roasted and then served with their feathers replaced; and chickens glazed with honey. There was certainly no shortage of ideas to tempt the palates of the rich. At a dinner given by a Parisian merchant, guests were offered a wide choice. The first course consisted of meat in a cinnamon sauce, pastries of cod liver or beef marrow, eels in a spicy purée, loach in a cold green sauce with sage, beef marrow fritters, joints of meat, saltwater fish, roast bream and *darioles*

(little savoury dishes), sturgeon and jellies. For the second course there were more roast meats, freshwater fish, broth with bacon, meat *tile* (sautéed chicken and veal, spiced sauce of powdered crayfish tails, almonds, and toasted bread, garnished with more crayfish tails), capon pasties and crisps, bream and eel pasties, and *blamanger* (a type of bread sauce). And, finally, the third course included *frumenty* (a porridge with raisins and honey), venison and lampreys with hot sauce. Guests were not expected to try every dish, however, and portions were not large.

As with many aspects of life throughout the Middle Ages, there was a great delight in the visual. On few occasions was this emphasis on presentation more pronounced than at the wedding of the English Prince Lionel, Duke of Clarence, to Violante, a daughter of the powerful Visconti family in Milan, in 1368. The banquet consisted of 30 complementary courses of meat and fish, from which guests would be

EARLY SWEETENER Labourers tend their beehives in 15th-century Milan. Honey was cheaper than sugar.

expected to have a taste of as many as they liked: suckling pig with crab, hare with pike, calf with trout, duck and heron with carp, beef and capons with sturgeon, beef pies with eel pies, and meat aspic with fish aspic. Side dishes included roasted kid, venison, peacocks with cabbage, beans and pickled ox-tongue, junkets, cheeses and fruit. The meats and fish were all gilded with a paste of powdered egg yolk, saffron and flour, to which gold leaf was added for the more flamboyant dishes. The leftovers from the vast meal were said to be enough to feed 1000 people. The bridegroom was immediately taken ill – some said from poison, some from indigestion. He never recovered and died four months later.

The basic diet of the European peasant was dark rye bread, cabbage, beans, a little salt pork, and curds, washed down with cider, water or ale. Ale was made from malt, water and spices, and was about as soupy as porridge: a skilled worker might drink as much as a gallon a day, costing a penny halfpenny or about a quarter of his daily wage (a cooked chicken would have cost twice that).

FOOD FOR THE POOR

In France in the mid-14th century two-thirds of the peasant's diet was bread, and less than an eighth consisted of fish or meat. Cheese was often the only source of protein for poor families, and it was not until the 14th century that wheat bread became a staple, even in the fertile plains of central Europe.

In many mountain areas, bread was made from rye or millet, and the basic dish was a soup made of root vegetables such as turnips, kohl rabi and earth artichokes, with perhaps some boiled legumes and a little goat's meat. In Ireland a similar basic meal was made of wild garlic, leeks, onions, peas and beans. Some of the meat and fish was smoked. Pork and herrings, on the other hand, were

WINE HARVEST Villagers in 15th-century France pick the fruit from the vines, while one man treads the grapes.

PEPPER AND SALT

In the Middle Ages, rich people placed large silver salt cellars on their dining tables. Those who sat on the lord's side of this cellar looked down on those who literally sat 'below the salt' – hence the origin of the phrase. During the Middle Ages, salt and spices were as negotiable as silver – which explains other phrases, such as 'worth his salt'.

Far from being a nominal sum as it is today, a peppercorn rent – about a pound of pepper – was the equivalent of a few weeks' agricultural labour.

soaked in brine and hung over a fire for a few days, which preserved them for months. In northern Europe, the Norwegian *stokkfish* was a source of protein: the cod was gutted, cut into strips and dried on wooden racks in the sun. The result took a while to reconstitute, according to a 14th-century recipe: 'it behoves to beat it with a wooden hammer for a full hour and then set it to soak in warm water for a full two hours or more, then cook it and scour it very well.' The dish was served with mustard or soaked in

butter. To soak up the salt in their food throughout the winter months, people added oatmeal, dried peas, dried beans, breadcrumbs and whole grains to their stews. Puréed beans with bacon became a standard dish throughout Europe. By the later Middle Ages, people had developed a taste for fried food, such as fish or eggs fried in olive or nut oil.

When there was enough to go round, this diet was healthier than that of the rich, though it lacked variety. Peasants poached what they could, risking death or maiming if they were caught. It was safer to gather nuts, mushrooms and edible snails from the woods and common land.

Not every nation ate the same food. Sir John Fortescue, writing in 1471, cast a critical eye over the French: 'They drink water, they eat apples, with brown bread made from rye; they eat no flesh unless it be very seldom a little lard, or the entrails or hides of beasts slain for the nobles and merchants of the land ... blessed be God, the people of this land [England] is ruled under a better law, and therefore the people thereof be not in such penury.'

CUSTOMS AND CUTLERY

In the towns, convenience food was popular. You could take bread dough or a small joint of meat to a communal oven for baking. Or you could buy ready-cooked pies and pasties from shops: in 1363, for example, a leg of roast mutton cost $2^1/2$d (a day's wage for an agricultural labourer).

Food was often adulterated in shops and markets.

KITCHEN SCENES Cooks and their assistants stir a stewpot, chop vegetables, pound food in a giant pestle and mortar, and finally carve the food for serving at table.

POTS AND PANS
English cooking utensils from the 14th and 15th centuries include two bronze cauldrons and a steel-bladed knife.

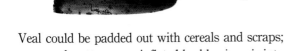

suppliers of cooking oil that had previously been used to bathe sufferers from venereal disease.

The basic eating implement was the knife, which you took with you if you were invited out to dinner. Spoons existed, but most liquid foods, such as soups and broths were supped straight from the bowl. Forks were unknown in Europe until the 14th century, when they appeared from the Near East in Greece, Italy, and then France. The popes in Avignon were among the first to possess forks, made of gold and crystal.

Plates were made of metal or wood, but for much of the period it was more common to use a large slice or 'trench' of stale bread. This is the origin of the phrase 'a good trencherman'. These trenches would be given to the dogs or the poor at the end of the meal.

Strict regulations governed fasting in Catholic Europe. Meat was prohibited during Lent, during the 30 days of Advent leading up to Christmas, on the eves of certain religious holidays, and – for part of the medieval period – on Mondays, Wednesdays and Fridays. Even in the 16th century, it was legally possible to be hanged for eating meat on a Friday in some northern European countries. In total, meat was off the menu for between 190 and 200 days a year.

Fasting was no bad thing. People ate more vegetables during Lent and Advent, as well as dried figs, dates, raisins, hazelnuts and walnuts. Some Lenten dishes were quite inventive. A popular dish in England was *ryschewys* – a mixture of figs, ale, almonds, pears, dates and fish all pounded into a paste, shaped into rissoles, floured, dipped in batter and fried in oil.

Veal could be padded out with cereals and scraps; carcasses of mutton were inflated by blowing air into them; kidneys were stuffed with rags; and ox fat was sewn on to other more expensive meat.

Sawdust was often sold as grated nutmeg; and dried juniper berries were substituted for more costly peppercorns. Similarly, customers were often cheated when fruit, vegetables and meat were weighed: a portion would be removed by sleight of hand as it was dispensed.

The problem got worse with the growth of the towns and the rise in the number of markets; and new regulations were introduced. Those caught tricking the public were paraded through the streets and locked in the pillory – to be pelted with rotten fruit.

In France special inspectors of pork were appointed, and *langueyeurs*, to check the tongues of animals for the ulcers that were said to cause leprosy. In Venice in 1498 a prosecution was brought against

DINNER GUESTS   A medieval lord dines with his family.

those older people who were less proud of their figures and wished to keep them hidden from view. During the Middle Ages, the practice of painting the face, which had been dormant since Roman times, was revived. Fashions varied from country to country: in Italy women used paint made from flour mixed with various dyes to make their faces look darker; in England and France the fashion was generally to appear pale – with some women even bleeding themselves regularly to achieve a suitably wan look. However, there were temporary swings. In the 11th century, English prostitutes painted their faces white, but the fashion later spread to noble-women. Once that happened, prostitutes began to use rouge to advertise their profession.

Face make-up consisted of a paint or paste. Dry pigments made from plant roots or leaves, or even crushed insects, were mixed with water in a flat dish, and the resulting paste was smeared on to the face with the fingers. A 13th-century verse listed the contents of a beauty tool-kit for women:

I have all the various things
A woman needs who would be fair:
Razors, forceps, mirrors too,
Combs and irons for her hair,
Picks and brushes for her teeth,
Bandeaux or a fancy pin.
Cotton to apply her rouge,
White enamel for her skin.

The rough-and-ready mixtures applied to the face often played havoc with a woman's skin. To undo the damage, recipes offered a variety of remedial ointments, such as one made by taking 'asparagus roots, wild anise, bulbs of

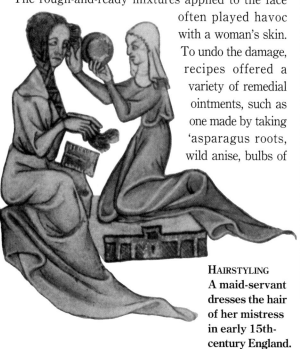

HAIRSTYLING
A maid-servant
dresses the hair
of her mistress
in early 15th-
century England.

DID YOU KNOW?

In 1449, Thomas Brightfield of London built a water closet that was flushed by water piped from a cistern. The invention never became popular, and over 400 years passed before Brightfield's flushing toilet was re-invented.

One medieval beauty treatment involved applying whole toads to the face. Most authorities, however, advised women to mince them before use.

FACE PACKS
This woman
beautifies
herself with
whole toads,
rather than
minced ones.

white lilies, milk of wild asses or red goats, aged in warm horse manure and filtered through felt'. Fashionable women in the 14th and 15th centuries plucked their eyebrows and hairline to heighten the forehead – a practice particularly condemned by the moralists. They lined the upper lids with black liquid made by mixing pigment and saliva, and then, with a small stick, applied shadows of brown, grey, blue-green or violet.

By the 15th century even more attention was being paid to beautifying the face. Mirrors were cheaper and better and not regarded, as they had been centuries before, as 'the devil's hiding place'. People became more conscious of how they looked and, consequently, there was an increase in beauty advice and in the number of recipes for cosmetics.

THE BODY BEAUTIFUL

Some books, such as *The Dialogue on the Beauty of Women*, by the Italian writer and former monk Agnolo Firenzuola, listed a complete catalogue of how a woman should look. The ideal woman was blessed with fine hair, a spacious forehead, curved and ebony eyebrows, dark-tan or nut-brown eyes, thin lashes, ears the colour of pale rubies, cheeks 'patched' with

PALE COMPLEXION The high forehead and pale complexion of this Flemish woman conform to the medieval ideal.

sunset vermilion, a narrow and slightly turned-up nose ('coloured but not red'), a small mouth vermilion in colour and showing not more than five or six of the upper teeth, and a long slender neck. A double chin was considered a sign of beauty, too. Since much of medieval life consisted of tough physical work, it was

63

with their fingers from communal plates and other people's hygiene was therefore a matter of particular personal concern. In castles, at least, people washed their hands on entering the dining hall.

Most books of manners consisted of little more than the rules of table discipline and cleanliness. Tannhäuser's *Hofzucht* ('Courtly Manners') of the 15th century ruled that a man of refinement should, for example, not slurp from his spoon, bite from a slice of bread and then dunk it in the communal dish, gnaw on a bone and put it back in the dish, blow his nose on the tablecloth, snort like a seal when eating, smack his lips like a 'Bavarian yokel', poke his ears or pick his nose at table.

In all countries, instructions were much the same. A guest should not loosen his belt at table, wipe his hands on his robe ('but rather let the air dry them'), place his elbows on the table, talk too much, dip food in the salt cellar, clean his teeth with his knife, spit on or over the table, or fall asleep at the table.

Other rules were more subtle. According to one German treatise on good manners, when two people shared a plate or a trencher of bread, 'you should always eat with the outside hand; if your companion sits on your right, eat with your left hand, and vice versa. Refrain from eating with both hands.' It was, however, considered good manners to hold a wine goblet with both hands when drinking, and it was permissible to lift the plate to the mouth when eating soups or sauces. Meat was to be picked up with three fingers only, never with the whole hand. Bread was not to be eaten before the meat was served, as this appeared greedy.

Many writers, including Tannhäuser in Germany and Fra Bonvicino da Riva in Italy, suggested that when people ate at table they should think of the poor and needy, for 'God will reward you if you treat them kindly.' Da Riva went on to advise that 'To snort like a salmon, gobble like a badger, and complain while eating – these three things are quite improper.'

The most famous writer on etiquette and manners was almost certainly Desiderius Erasmus, the 16th-century Dutch humanist. In one of two treatises on the subject, *Diversoria*, he gave a lively description of an

WEDDING BREAKFAST The fare is plentiful, and the guests are hungry, at this Flemish peasant wedding feast, painted by Pieter Brueghel the Elder.

evening at a German inn. Some 80 or 90 people were crowded into one large room which was dirty and smelt of garlic and cooking. A group of women washed their clothes in a bucket and hung the dripping articles over a wood stove, which hissed steam into the smoky room. Men cleaned the mud from their boots at the table, and spat on the floor and table. As soon as the meal was served, everyone rushed to the table, dipping their bread and their fingers in the common dishes and the mustard pot, stuffing their mouths with more food before they had finished one mouthful, and splashing beads of sweat into the food. Erasmus criticised all such behaviour, and had one final piece of advice: 'Do not move back and forth on your chair, it gives the impression of constantly breaking or trying to break wind.'

At the other extreme were the formal dinners held at court or in the Hall of a great castle. In 15th-century France, at the home of the Duc de Berry, such meals began with a procession of dishes led by the 'grand master of the palace', bearing the staff of his office. Every dish was presented before the duke, and tasted in his presence. The chief carver then touched his carving knife with his lips and kissed the duke's napkin before slicing the meat. The table was laid with a centrepiece of a large ceremonial salt cellar covered with a napkin. Such salt cellars were sometimes decorated with 'serpents' tongues' – fossilized shark's teeth, which were believed to sweat if anything poisonous was placed near them. Beside the

ANCIENT ALLIANCE **King John I of Portugal entertains John of Gaunt (on the king's right), whose daughter married into the Portuguese royal family.**

salt cellar was the duke's bread, rolled in two napkins, and a goblet of wine, also covered. The cupbearer and breadmaster carried napkins over their shoulders while they served the duke, but had to lower their napkins when they moved on to serve persons of lesser rank. The gradations of society were strictly observed at table, and it was considered a great honour to sit on the duke's side of the salt cellar. The table was covered with two cloths: a richly embroidered undercloth that reached to the ground at both ends of the table, and an upper cloth that was the same size as the table top. A belt of linen (called a *samap*) was unrolled on the table to protect the cloth while guests washed their hands.

'YOUR FINGERNAILS SHOULD NOT BE TOO LONG'

❛ Your dress should be clean and without filth. Do not let your face or your hands be dirty. Take care that no drippings from the nose hang there like icicles that one sees hanging from the rafters and eaves of houses in winter. Your fingernails should not be too long or full of filth. Make sure that your hair is well combed and that your headdress is not full of feathers or other trash. Your shoes should be clean and not dirty or muddy. Your tongue should not be covered with filth. Have your teeth clean and without rust – that is to say, without the yellow matter attached to them as a result of insufficient cleansing. Understand that it is improper and discourteous to scratch your head on the table; to remove from your neck fleas or other vermin and kill them in front of others; to scratch or pull at scabs in whatever part of the body they may be. If you have to blow your nose, you should not remove the excrement with the fingers, but in a handkerchief. And if you spit or cough, you need not swallow what you have already drawn into the throat, but spit on the ground or into a handkerchief or napkin. If you are forced to belch, do so as quietly as possible, always averting the face. ❜

From *Basic Principles of Cleanliness*, Jean de Sulpice, 1483

THE MIDDLE AGES AT WORK

Leisure was unknown for most people – work began as soon as it was light and

continued until it was too dark to see. Tailors, masons, carpenters,

farmers, weavers, bakers, tanners, millers – modern surnames bear witness to

the vast range of skills and labours of the industrious Middle Ages.

There was work for all, and everyone was expected to take part –

husbands, wives and children.

LIFE ON THE LAND

'Poor folk in hovels, charged with children and overcharged by landlords,'

was the 14th-century poet William Langland's account of the peasant's life.

There was often little food and no comfort, but there was always plenty of work.

HE MIDDLE AGES were the age of muscle power, when most work was done by hand or on foot: tilling the soil; trudging behind the plough; cutting and dragging timber; spinning and weaving cloth; and making hurdles to pen sheep.

For the nine out of ten people who worked directly on the land, life was a constant battle against nature. This was equally true of the serf, sometimes the slave of the lord of the manor; the freeman, who either owned or leased his land, but did not belong to the lord; and the villein, who was somewhere in between the first two. In any case, by the 15th century, there was less of a distinction between the various classes of peasant, since – from economic necessity rather than a sense of equality – most peasants were free, paying rent for their lands to the lord rather than labour.

At times of good harvests, villagers had the energy and funds to clear new tracts of land and to plant more crops. After a couple of rainy summers or one of the many recurring outbreaks of plague, however, there was neither the will nor the manpower to keep nature at bay. During the Middle Ages in Europe, tens of thousands of villages disappeared forever as a result of war, disease or famine.

The Middle Ages were also a time of great climatic

FARMING YEAR A 15th-century manual shows different tasks: scything, ploughing, sheep-shearing and wood-cutting.

A SERF ON A WINTER'S DAY IN 12TH-CENTURY ENGLAND

GODRIC woke before first light. He could hear and feel the rain dripping through the turf roof of his hut, heralding another cold, wet, hard day's work. He pulled on his grubby woollen tunic over the clothes he had slept in, tied a bundle of rags round his feet, and hurried out to the fields, for he knew the bailiff would be out there marking down the names of anyone late to start work on the lord's ploughing.

Goading the oxen and directing the scratch plough over the damp, heavy soil was vile work in this weather, but Godric knew that only if he performed this task satisfactorily would he be allowed the use of the lord's ox team one day a week to plough the strips of land he rented for his own use.

When the bell from the village church rang for the Sanctus later in the morning, Godric rested a moment and ate the crust of bread he had snatched up as he left the hut. There was time for a few words with other serfs working in the same field, the main topic of conversation being yesterday's hue and cry. A poacher had been seen on the edge of the forest, with a rabbit in a snare. The hue and cry had been raised by the lord's reeve, so every peasant had stopped work and given chase. The poacher had been seized and dragged to the village lock-up. Godric had been one of those posted to guard him for part of the night. The poor devil would be sentenced at the Manor Court tomorrow – a fine if he had the money, a whipping and worse if he had not. All that had lost a good two hours' work.

Ploughing was not the only task Godric had to perform for his lord. There was hedging and ditching, and dung-spreading; pigs and cattle to be driven to market, for there was little fodder left to feed them through the winter; walls and fences had to be repaired; rushes had to be collected and then taken over to the manor to cover the floor in the Great Hall. All this – and little daylight in which to do it.

It would be a busy day for Godric at the Manor Court tomorrow, for he planned to put forward a plea to take over the land of the widow Reynberd. She was unable to work the land herself, and Godric hoped to persuade the reeve and the lord's cellarer to grant him his request, and not to ask for too great a sum of money to enter the land in his name.

At three in the afternoon, Godric stopped work. At this time of year, the light would soon be gone; he had to return the oxen to his lord's stable, and there was work of his own to do. The pig would need feeding, and he was hungry for the meal of soft cheese, sour bread and a broth of dried beans that his wife should have ready for him. As he settled onto his straw mattress, Godric prayed that the rain would stop.

KILLING A PIG
A man uses the flat back of an axe blade to smash the animal's skull, around 1150.

change in Europe. From the middle of the 8th century until the early 13th century, the climate was mild and dry: to such an extent that vineyards prospered in northern England; land was ploughed to a higher altitude than ever before (or since), and Viking colonies in Greenland pastured cattle in luxuriant green meadows. But between 1215 and 1350 the climate changed. Icebergs moved south from the Arctic and the average temperature dropped by two or three degrees, which was enough to kill vines and lower the tree line on the mountains.

The introduction in the 13th century of a new system of crop rotation compensated for this climatic change, increasing food production by nearly a third. The 'three field system' did not work for the whole of Europe, however. The soil was drier and stonier in Italy, Spain, Greece and Sicily, and there was too little rain to support more than one arable crop a year. Furthermore, the soil had already been farmed for up to 2000 years and had lost much of its richness; farmers had to rely on olives, vines and fruit trees to provide other harvests.

PLOUGHING, SOWING AND HARVESTING

The hardest part of life on the land was preparing the ground for the autumn or spring sowing. In the poorest parts of Europe, there were no draught animals, and a man and his wife pushed and pulled the simple scratch plough themselves. Any hard lumps of soil were broken with small hammers: back-breaking work that was undertaken by the whole family. After this, the land was smoothed and levelled with a rake, or with a harrow in villages lucky enough to have one. Children followed the harrow, plucking stones from the earth.

When the land was ready for sowing, peasants strapped small wooden boxes, full of seed, to their shoulders, and walked to and fro, up and down the strips of land, scattering the seed by hand. In the more advanced agricultural areas of northern Europe, oxen or (for better-off farmers) horses pulled the superior

mouldboard plough, which cut horizontally as well as vertically into the earth, and turned each slice of soil over, thus exposing the roots of any weeds.

At harvest time, the lord of the manor had the right to decide on which days the peasants were to work bringing in his harvest. Peasants sweated on the lord's land through the best days, praying that the fine weather would hold long enough for them to gather in their own crops.

Women helped in the fields, but they also had plenty to do at home. As soon as the animals had been turned out of the cottage first thing in the morning, the women swept the earth floor, put away the straw

---

A DAY IN THE LIFE OF

A FREEMAN ON A SUMMER'S DAY IN 14TH-CENTURY FRANCE

GERVASE rose early, as soon as the sunlight filtered through the oiled muslin sheets that served as the windows of his cottage. He woke his sons, breakfasted off a hunk of bread and a draught of ale, and went out to the fields. Although it was Sunday, the priest of Gervase's village allowed his parishioners to work, so long as they stopped in time for morning Mass.

Gervase and his sons passed the stone cross at the edge of the village, crossing themselves almost without thinking, and arrived at the meadow. Gervase and his eldest son, Mark, sharpened their scythes on a whetstone and set to work cutting the long grass.

They worked steadily for three hours or more and then returned to the cottage, to change into their best clothes for Mass in the tiny village church. The whole family set off together, and Gervase noticed that where the wall round the graveyard

CUTTING CORN **Throughout Europe, men and women worked together to gather the harvest.**

needed repair, cattle had been able to clamber into the graveyard and graze on the graves. The family entered the church, dipping their fingers into the font of holy water and once more making the sign of the cross.

The service was in Latin, which none of them understood. Gervase let his mind wander as he stood on the stone floor. Occasionally he joined in a murmured conversation with his neighbours, and even shared a joke. The news was that there was

a swarm of bees in the woods, and Gervase promised to join his neighbours the next day, beating an iron pot with a thick stick, so that the bees would think thunder was in the air and seek the shelter of a hive before the rain started.

Back at home, Gervase left the cooking and housework to his wife and daughter, and went to the close at the back of the cottage to feed his pig with sour milk and kitchen scraps. He spent a little time weeding his garden, and wondering how well his second son, Richard, was managing their flock of sheep on the hillside a few miles away. Only last week one of his neighbour's cows had wandered over another's land and had been placed in the village pound by the reeve.

In the afternoon, the family continued hay-making. After an evening meal of meat and bread, cheese and ale, Gervase retired to his feather-mattressed bed.

'SUCH A NOISE OF NESTLING'

THESE LINES (in modern translation) are taken from a poem, *Richard the* | *Redeless*, written around 1400. They celebrate the author's native country- | side – probably the English West Midlands – in the summertime.

I turned me twice and looked about,
Beholding hedges and woods so green,
The mansions and meadows mown all new,
For such was the season of the same year.
The flowers in fields smelling sweet,
The corn on the crofts cropped full fair,
The running river rushing fast,
Full of fish and of fry of manifold kind,
The briars with their berries bent over the ways,
As honeysuckles hanging upon each half,

Chestnuts and cherries that children desire
Were lodged under leaves full lusty to be seen.
Pears and plums and peascods green,
That ladies lusty look much after
Were gathered for men ere they were ripe …
And so down to the dale, dwelled I no longer,
But such a noise of nestling nor so sweet notes
I heard not this half year, nor so heavenly sounds
As I did on that dale down among the hedges.

mattresses and the truckle beds, fed the geese and chickens, and settled down to the housework. There was always baking and cooking to be done, though meals were fairly simple. At least once every two or three weeks, most women brewed the family's ale. Dirty clothes were very occasionally taken to the stream or river and pounded against stones. Milk from cows, or more often from sheep, was turned into cheese and butter.

Any time left over was used to spin woollen thread and weave rough cloth; it was to this end that women often took spindles with them into the fields when they minded the pigs or fed the cattle. Small hand looms for weaving tended to be shared. Once a large enough piece of cloth had been made, it was taken to the river to be trampled in water. This thickened the cloth and made it shrink. The cloth was then dyed with a mixture of vegetable dyes, after

which it was pressed with a hot iron and trimmed with metal shears, before being roughly tailored at home to provide a tunic or cloak.

Children were expected to share in all aspects of work, scaring birds from the fields, weeding, looking after geese and chickens, shepherding small flocks of sheep, and driving pigs into the forest to grub for acorns and beech mast. They also scavenged for nuts and berries, collected edible plants and roots, provided a continuous supply of rushes for lamps, and took part in the never-ending collection of firewood and furze for the cottage fire.

The one worker who escaped the close control of the lord of the manor and his many agents was the shepherd. For much of Europe the sheep was the most commercially attractive animal: raw wool and woollen cloth were England's most valuable exports; the entire economy of Flanders was founded on the wool trade; sheep's milk provided the basic

TO PLOUGH AND SOW
Only wealthy peasants could afford teams of horses. Here the horses pull a harrow to break up the ploughed land.

FINE-WEATHER WORK
English labourers stack corn sheaves.

A Village at Harvest-Time

Villages in the Middle Ages were practically self-sufficient economic units. As well as the lord of the manor, the local priest and agricultural labourers, most villages, such as this one in 13th-century England, contained a miller, a blacksmith, a wheelwright, a carpenter and joiner, a cooper and possibly a thatcher or tiler, too. Village life revolved around the twin centres of the parish church and the manor house, complete with its great hall.

The local miller (top right) had the monopoly of grinding the corn, and charged for his work by taking a percentage of the flour produced. The smith not only shod horses, but also made and repaired farm tools from the simple adze, used to hack at the soil, to the more complicated plough and harrow; he also mended pots and pans, and made knives, chains, bolts and locks, and swords and spearheads in times of war. The carpenter and joiner made the wooden frames of ploughs, spade and sickle handles, yokes for the ox harness, and the timber cruck frames for the villagers' cottages.

Apart from the land which was farmed directly by the lord of the manor, and the glebeland (which was farmed by the local priest), most fields were divided into strips, roughly 180 yards long and 5 or 6 yards wide – the length being determined by how far a pair of oxen could pull a plough without needing a rest. The land owned or rented by any one peasant would consist of several of these strips, each was separated from the other and spread over several fields. There was also some common land where the villagers grazed their sheep and cattle.

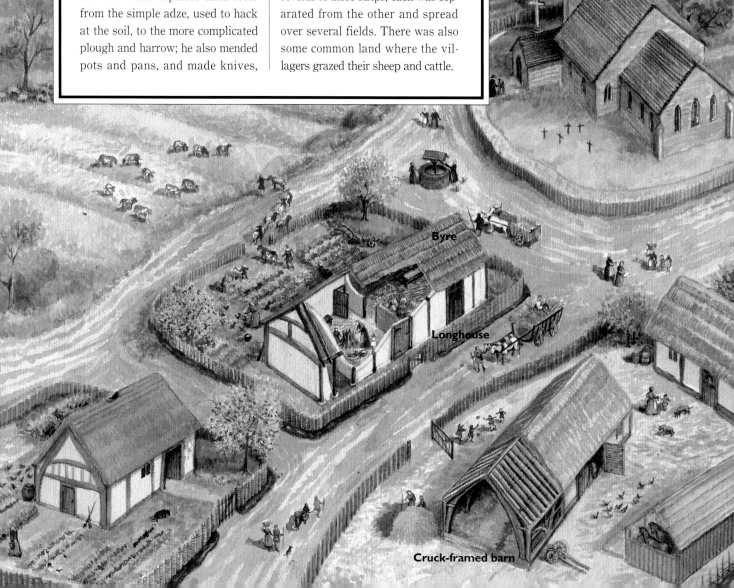

Byre

Longhouse

Cruck-framed barn

Manor house

Village stocks

Blacksmith

Potter

Common land

Beehives

Building a wattle fence

Harvesting

75

THE PEASANTS' REVOLT

ONE RESULT of the Black Death and the other outbreaks of plague in the 14th century was an acute shortage of labour. Peasants began to demand more money for their work, and in some countries laws were passed to limit wages to pre-plague levels. At the same time, people had to pay taxes in order to raise money for the wars that raged throughout France, Germany, Italy and Spain.

Revolution was in the air. In 1358 the French peasantry took up arms, declaring that their lords had 'shamed and despoiled the realm, and it would be a good thing to destroy them all'. Castles were looted and burnt, and a score or so of nobles were killed. Similar uprisings took place in Florence in 1378 and in Ghent a year later.

The largest and most dangerous revolt was in England in 1381. A poll tax of four pence for all lay people over the age of 14 had been introduced to raise money for the wars with France. In late May whole villages in Kent and Essex refused to pay. They armed themselves with rusty swords and axes, longbows, knives, sickles and pitchforks. Having elected Wat Tyler and Jack Straw as their leaders, they marched towards London, releasing John Ball from prison. For 20 years, Ball had

REVOLUTIONARY Kentish peasants such as this man joined the rebels in their thousands.

SMITHFIELD, 1381 Richard II is shown twice in this picture. On the left, he watches the Lord Mayor of London kill Wat Tyler. On the right, he addresses the armed peasants, and offers himself as Tyler's replacement.

been preaching that all men were equal – 'When Adam delved and Eve span,' he asked 'who was then the gentleman?'

He also asked for the lands of the Church to be confiscated and shared among the poor: 'My good friends, matters cannot go well in England until all things shall be in common; when there shall be neither vassals nor lords ... They are clothed in velvet and rich stuffs, while we are forced to wear poor clothing. They have wines, spices and fine bread, while we only have rye and the refuse of the straw ... They have handsome seats and manors, while we must brave the wind and rain in our labours in the field; and it is by our labour they have the wherewithal to support their pomp.'

This ragged army reached the outskirts of London on June 13, 1381, where they killed the Archbishop of Canterbury and put a series of demands. Richard II was only 14 years old, but he rode out to Smithfield to negotiate. He promised

to meet their demands: an end to serfdom, abolition of the poll tax, free use of the forests, free pasturage, free fishing rights and an end to the game laws.

Accounts as to what happened next are confused. Perhaps in self-defence, William Walworth, Mayor of London, rode up to Wat Tyler and plunged his sword into the rebel's breast. There were roars of rage and dismay from the peasants, at which the king bravely spurred his horse and rode among them saying: 'I am your captain. I am your King. Quiet yourselves.' Once the moment for revolution had passed, the king's army surrounded the peasants' camp. Wat Tyler's head was displayed on the point of a lance – to show that the leader of the rising was dead and as a warning to others.

The peasants dispersed, to be hounded by troops. Many were imprisoned, and a few, including John Ball, were put to death. All the promises made to the insurgents by the king were broken.

CHURCH TAX Tithes were stored in barns like this one at Widdington in Essex. A peasant reaps his harvest (above right); others hand over their tithes (right).

protein in the peasant diet from Scotland to Sicily, Portugal to Poland; and in south-west France and southern Spain, wool and sheepskins even took the place of money in many communities. As pastoral farming became more profitable than arable farming, landed estates invested heavily in huge flocks of sheep. Fountains Abbey, for example, had 19,000 and was partly responsible – along with other monasteries – for turning large tracts of England into moorland.

By 1350 there were probably fewer than 2 million people in England – scattered at a density of roughly 40 people per square mile – with sheep far outnumber-

'I SAW A POOR MAN HANGING ONTO THE PLOUGH'

❛ As I went by the way, weeping for sorrow, I saw a poor man hanging on to the plough. His coat was of coarse stuff which was called cary; his hood was full of holes and his hair stuck out of it. As he trod the soil his toes peered out of his worn shoes with their thick soles; his hose hung about his hocks on all sides, and he was be-daubed with mud as he followed the plough. He had two mittens, made scantily of rough stuff, with worn-out fingers and thick with muck. This man bemired himself in the mud almost to the ankle, and drove four heifers before him that had become feeble, so that men might count their every rib so sorry looking they were.

His wife walked beside him with a long goad in a shortened cote-hardy [thick coat] looped up full high and wrapped in a winnowing sheet to protect her from the weather. She went barefoot on the ice so that the blood flowed. At the end of the row lay a little crumb bowl, and therein a little child covered with rags, and two two-year-olds were on the other side, and they all sang one song that was pitiful to hear: they all cried the same cry – a miserable note. The poor man sighed sorely, and said "Children be still". ❜

From *Piers the Plowman*, probably by William Langland, late 14th century

ing humans. That is why, in the 16th century, Sir Thomas More would write that 'sheep … have become so great devourers … that they eat up the very men themselves.'

Wool brought fortunes to many traders and merchants, but it provided little more than an adequate living for the men who actually tended the sheep. In the uplands of Europe, shepherds led nomadic lives throughout the summer months, driving large flocks of sheep across hundreds of miles, from pasture to pasture, and from one country to another. They constituted an irregular brotherhood, owing allegiance to their calling and to each other rather than to any lord or nation. Indeed, it was said that the migrant shepherd changed his master more often than his shirt.

They sheltered in huts and cabins – often little more than rough stone walls offering some defence against the bears, wolves and lynxes that still roamed much of Europe. Here, the shepherds shared the daily tasks of cooking and cheese-making, and established informal co-operatives. They kept no written accounts, but they knew exactly how many sheep were under their control at any one time. Much of the time they and their flocks were trespassing over the land of other lords, but the bribe of a fleece or two was enough to placate the agents sent after them.

Some of the shepherds were away from home for only a few days at a time, coming down from the hills for supplies of bread and wine at regular intervals. Others were away for months or even years on end, moving from one adventure and one woman to another, setting up special cabins for the winter months, with kitchen areas, corners for hanging clothes, and separate bedrooms. In many ways they lived more comfortably than their brothers and sisters back home in the village.

Lambing sometimes took place as early as

WOMAN'S WORK
Above: a woman releases a ferret into a burrow, while her companion traps the escaping rabbit in her net.
Right: another milks a cow.

Christmas time; in the spring the lambs were weaned and milking began; and in the summer the flocks moved to the higher pastures. Shearing took place on the open hillsides, and the fleeces were transported back to the valleys on teams of mules and asses. It was a routine as old as the hills themselves.

THE WINDMILL AND THE WATERMILL

To supplement all that hard physical labour, the people of the Middle Ages also used a surprising number of machines, the commonest of which was the mill. Mills were used for grinding corn, fulling cloth – that is, scouring, cleaning and thickening it by beating it in water – for tanning leather and even for making paper. One water-powered mill could do the work of 40 people and did not need to rest at night. Once the efficiency and profitability of mills had been realised, hundreds of thousands were built right across Europe.

In the 12th century medieval engineers began to construct windmills, adopting yet another innovation brought to Europe by the returning Crusaders. The initial problem in Europe was that, whereas streams always flow in the same direction, the wind constantly changes direction. This had not been a problem in the Middle East, where the wind blows steadily in one direction for most of the year. The solution to the European problem was the invention of the post-mill, in which the entire framework of the mill is mounted on a massive upright oak post, so that it swivels to catch the wind from any direction.

THE HORSE AND THE OX

For centuries, the ox had been almost the only draught animal in Europe. It was cheaper to feed than a horse, cost less to buy, and required less care and attention. With the development of harnesses from the late 12th century and heavier horseshoes, however, farmers discovered that the horse was capable of 30 per cent more work, simply

MEDIEVAL TECHNOLOGY
This 14th-century post-mill uses a tree stump as an axis so that it can be turned to face the wind.

because it could move faster than the ox while pulling a plough. Nevertheless, both the animals had their supporters and their champions. A leading English agriculturalist, Walter of Henley, argued that the ox was the superior animal since it ate only two shillings and eightpence worth of feed in a winter, while a horse ate eight shillings and twopence worth of oats, and that 'when the horse is old and worn out then hath he nothing but his skin – but when the ox is old with tenpence worth of grass he will be made fat to kill or to sell for as much as he cost you.'

Many peasants could not afford a horse, and there were vast areas of southern Europe where the climate and soil were unsuitable for growing oats, the horse's winter feed. Throughout the rest of Europe, however, the horse gradually replaced the ox. When harnessed in pairs, and with better carts, horses were capable of an impressive work load. Every day, when Troyes Cathedral was under construction in the 13th century, each pair of horses pulled a wagon weighing

SHEPHERDS HEY! **A Dutch book of hours from the mid-15th century shows a group of dancing shepherds.**

THE FARMING YEAR

Winter

The year began with the back-breaking task of preparing the soil for next season's crops. The land was ploughed and harrowed to break up large lumps of soil, and planted with wheat, oats or rye in northern Europe, and with wheat or corn in southern Europe. It was also a time for the miserable task of slaughtering all those animals for whom there would be insufficient winter feed. The meat from these carcasses was then salted, pickled, smoked or cured. If there was no other work to be done, time was spent mending tools and equipment.

Spring

There was more ploughing to be done. Hedges were cut low to encourage a new, thicker growth. Fruit trees were pruned. Sheep and cattle that had been overwintered were turned out of their winter quarters to graze, and to manure that part of the land that was being left fallow. Peas and beans were planted. The first pickings of fresh herbs were taken for the kitchen and medicine chest. Some fields and strips were marled – a heavier, richer soil was added to improve the fertility of the soil and the crop yield.

Summer

Hay-making began in June. The meadow was cut with scythes and the hay turned regularly with pitchforks to make sure that it would dry thoroughly before being raked into haycocks. It was a busy time for the hayward, who had to make sure that all cattle were kept away from the young shoots of wheat, barley, oats or rye. Vegetables were harvested – peas, beans, a few greens, but no root crops. Honey was collected from the hives, and fish and eels were taken from river and stream.

Autumn

This was the busiest time of year. The fields were cut and the sheaves of corn collected. Threshing to separate the corn from the straw was done by beating it with flails on the floor of the barn (if there was one – in the open if there was not). Flails were two sticks hinged together with eelskins. Winnowing (separating the grain from the chaff) was left to the women of the village, who tossed the corn high into the air from large straw baskets, letting the wind blow away the chaff and catching the corn in the baskets as it fell. The first corn was taken to the mill to be ground into flour. Nuts and berries were gathered from the heathland and woods. Apples, quinces and pears were picked in the orchards. Wood was gathered and stored beside the cottages. Any spare time was used to make candles or rush dips for the long winter nights.

$2^1/2$ tons and loaded with a further $2^1/2$ tons of stone from the quarries to the cathedral, a distance of over 30 miles.

VILLAGE LIFE AND DEATH

A bad summer was inevitably followed by a bad harvest and the certainty of a winter of hunger. In the 12th century alone, there were at least 20 years when the crops failed and famine struck Europe – in Portugal, Spain, Germany, France, the Low Countries and England.

Apart from recurrent hunger and perennial discomfort, villagers were at all times hosts to lice and fleas, and a variety of internal and external parasites such as whip-worms and ringworm, especially after a mild winter. They were victims of illness and diseases, such as pneumonia, tuberculosis (known simply as 'spitting blood'), epilepsy (known as the 'falling sickness'), itch, leprosy, scabies, rabies, scrofula, ulcers, abscesses, St Anthony's fire and St Martial's fire (an itching and inflammation of the skin, now known as erysipelas, often leading to a loss of sensation in the fingers and toes, and possibly gangrene).

Not surprisingly, peasants all over Europe needed to be tough to survive. The *Geste de Garin de Lorrain*, written in the 12th century, described the typical medieval peasant as having 'enormous arms, huge limbs, eyes a hand's breadth apart, broad shoulders, an enormous chest, bristling hair and a face as black as coal. He went six months without washing. The only water that ever touched his face was the rain.'

Even without visits from the plague, death struck every medieval village with great regularity. Most children died in infancy; many women died in childbirth, and the average life expectancy was very low indeed. Everyone, noble and peasant alike, was aware of the nearness of death, and all attempted to be prepared for this moment by seeking the grace of God and absolution for their sins. When news spread that a villager was dying, the women gathered at the dying person's cottage and the priest was sent for. The death itself was followed by a ritual lament, the tolling of the church bell and a rapid burial. In the words of an anonymous 13th-century poet:

HORSEPOWER A team of horses pulls a harvest cart up a hill. When Troyes Cathedral in France (above) was being built in the 13th century, a pair of horses would haul tons of stone daily for over 30 miles.

Remember that thou shall die,
For this world in certainty
Hath nothing save death truly.
Therefore in thy mind use this lesson:
Live so that death take thee in season.

The simple stones and wooden crosses in the graveyard were a constant reminder of the frailty of man, since there was scarcely a day in the life of any peasant when he did not pass the graves of his parents, grandparents and great-grandparents. He was thus reminded also of the continuity of the generations.

TRADERS AND TOWNSPEOPLE

Crowded, noisy, stinking, bustling and often riotous – medieval towns were

trading posts for merchants and manufacturers, sanctuaries for runaway serfs,

hunting grounds for thieves and rogues, and centres of political and spiritual power.

OWNS GREW UP where roads met, where rivers could be bridged or forded, where there was a natural harbour, or around religious sites. They were lively, noisy, crowded places where sellers of soap, garlic, coal, fish, meat, spices, flour, fur, pitch, tallow, iron, salt, grindstones, pots and pans, horses, armour, linen, oil, honey and nails plied their wares; and where papal agents, knights, friars, merchants, pedlars, chapmen (travelling salesmen), minstrels, buffoons, ballad-singers and pilgrims halted in their journeys. But the real wealth and security of any town was its trade. Lords granted leading citizens, or burgesses, the right to purchase charters of freedom from any tolls and customs dues that hindered trade. Once a charter had been granted to a town, the burgesses and town council were able to regulate trading conditions there – in effect, turning the town into a little pocket of freedom within the feudal system.

THE LAYOUT OF THE MEDIEVAL TOWN

Surrounded by fortified walls with heavy gates, the streets of a typical medieval town were dark and dank, narrow, winding and noisy, and constructed from cobbles or beaten dirt. People thronged them from sunrise to sunset, dodging the contents of chamber pots hurled from upstairs windows onto the streets. Horse-drawn carts and wagons with iron-rimmed wheels clattered up and down; packs of mules loaded with panniers of merchandise picked their way

---

EYEWITNESS

'SHE WATCHES OVER THE WHOLE HOUSE'

❛ The good housewife is one who looks to everything in the house. She takes care of the granary and keeps it clean so that no filth can enter. She sees to the oil jars, bearing in mind, this is to be thrown away and that kept ... she sees to the salted meat, both in the salting and the preserving. She cleans the meat, and decides this is to be sold and that kept. She causes the flax to be spun, and the linen to be woven ... She sells the bran and with the profits she gets the linen out of pawn. She looks to the wine barrels, if any are broken or leaky. She watches over the whole house. ❜

**San Bernardino,
15th-century Italian preacher**

HOUSEWIFELY DUTY An Italian townswoman of the 14th century draws vinegar from a keg.

❛ Tomorrow morning send back the small jar of dried raisins and the bread, by Namin of Santa Chiara. And send the barrel of vinegar ... Remember to wash the mule's feet with hot water down to her hoofs, and have her well-fed and cared for. And have my hose made and then soled by Meo ... And give some of the millet that is left with you to the nag, and see that it is well mashed ... And hasten the sale of the two barrels of wine in Bettina's house; and fill all the other vats in the cellar, with the white wine that has already been opened. ❜

**Letter from Francesco de Marco
Datini to his wife Margherita**

EXPORT IMPORT The port of Hamburg, seen in this 15th-century picture, was a thriving centre for trade.

mongers, vintners, skinners, salters, leathersellers, ironmongers, glovemakers, tailors and needlemakers.

In the centre of the town stood the homes of the wealthier merchants, the guildhalls and the market-place. This was where major commercial decisions were taken and where the town had a chance to flaunt its civic wealth and pride in handsome buildings, statues and fountains. Tucked away down narrow side alleys were the stables and 'lay stalls' (storage sites for refuse and dung), and the hovels of the poor artisans and labourers.

The towns also sheltered a shifting population of sailors, soldiers of fortune, Jews, messengers, envoys and drifters from all over Europe. Their numbers were swollen by refugees from the feudalism of the countryside, since a serf could gain his freedom if he stayed in a town for a year and a day. However, one ex-serf, Simon de Paris, a member of the Mercers' Guild and an alderman of the City of London, found it was dangerous to leave town even after he had lived there for 20 years. He made the mistake of visiting the village of his youth and serfdom, only to be arrested. It took him three years to prove to the local justices that he had a valid right to freedom.

The greatest change in medieval society came with the rise in the 14th and 15th centuries of the merchants, who broke with feudal tradition and the teaching of the Church to pursue money-making as an

between the crowds; and apprentices shouted their masters' wares, although it was illegal to tout for custom once a customer had entered a rival shop. Town criers marched from street to street, calling out news of the latest bankruptcies, of dealings in the city, or reports of lost cattle or stolen goods. Added to all this turmoil, there were animals everywhere: dogs and cats; rodents; sheep and cattle being driven to market; and stray pigs rooting in the piles of refuse to be found at every corner.

Metal signs hung from the shops, with pictures of the crafts practised there. Craftsmen and dealers in each trade usually had premises in the same street, for mutual protection and co-operation, and to keep an eye on each other. As a consequence, streets were often named after specific trades: mercers, drapers, goldsmiths, grocers, fish-

METALWORKERS Tools were simple, but medieval gold- and silversmiths still managed to produce some exquisite specimens of their art.

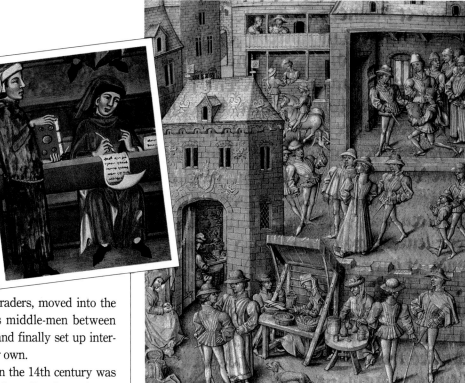

end in itself. The early Church Fathers, as severe in their condemnation of commerce as of sex, had claimed that money was evil and that usury, or money-lending for interest, was a sin. Their teachings, however, did as little to suppress capitalist enterprise as concupiscence, as many of the most successful merchants started their careers as retail traders, moved into the wholesale market – acting as middle-men between producers and shopkeepers – and finally set up international trading houses of their own.

Francesco di Marco Datini in the 14th century was one of the most successful of all medieval merchants, with trading houses all over Europe. He dealt in lead, alum and pilgrims' robes from Romania; cloves and slaves from the Black Sea; wool from England; salt from Ibiza; silk and glass from Venice; leather from Córdoba and Tunis; wheat from Sardinia and Sicily; oranges, dates, bark and wine from Catalonia; buffalo and sheep hides from Pisa; and woad from Genoa.

At the age of 15 he had left his native Prato in Italy and travelled to Avignon with 150 florins in his pocket (about £15). Thirty-six years later, he returned a wealthy man to Prato, where he joined the guild of silk merchants. He opened a trading house in Florence and began dealing in luxury items with Paris: Tuscan silks, embroideries, pictures and Spanish jewels.

IN THE NAME OF GOD AND PROFIT

Datini had his own corps of messengers crisscrossing Europe on foot (up to 25 miles a day) and horseback (up to 50 a day), his own clerks, lawyers, accountants, cashiers, shop boys and office boys. Whenever necessary, he chartered convoys of ships to collect goods from England, France and the Mediterranean, often paying for an escort of armed war galleys. Furthermore, he insured everything in which he dealt against 'act of God, of the sea, of man, of fire, of jettison, of confiscation by princes or cities or any other person, of reprisal, mishap or any other impediment' – and he could afford to pay the high premium of 5.9 per cent of the value of the goods.

TRADING ACCOUNTS Street traders do brisk business at the gate of a French city (above). Clerks are hard at work in 15th-century Italy (above left).

Datini's average profit was 15–20 per cent. He worked long hours every day of his life, just as Leon Battista Alberti, a 15th-century Florentine humanist, would later endorse: 'It befits a merchant always to have ink-stained hands.' Datini was also a profoundly religious man. On the front page of every new trading

DID YOU KNOW?

Dick Whittington (who died in 1423) really did become Lord Mayor of London, but he did not acquire a cat until a statue was carved of him 150 years after his death.

London was the first city to suffer officially from air pollution. In 1285 people complained about coal fumes from the limekilns – producing lime for building and farming – in Southwark, Wapping and East Smithfield. A royal proclamation forbade the burning of coal.

The highest structure in any city in medieval Europe was the spire of Strasbourg Cathedral in Alsace, which rose to 466 feet – the height of a 44-storey skyscraper.

ledger that he opened he wrote in a hopeful attempt to reconcile Christianity and commerce: 'In the Name of God and of Profit!'

There were others like him: for example, the men who ran the Florentine banking houses of Bardi, Peruzzi, Acciaiuoli and Frescobaldi, which lent money to the warlike rulers of Europe. They also provided a comprehensive banking service, including letters of payment (an early form of traveller's cheque) and bills of exchange. Another reason for their success was that in 1252 Florence began to mint gold coins – florins – which gradually replaced earlier silver coinage as Europe's leading currency. In the 15th century, you could buy a reasonable-sized house for about 870 florins, and a horse for 42.

Another key development was in book-keeping. In its simplest form, medieval accounting involved recording cash receipts and payments, and measuring the resulting balance at the end of a period or of some specific venture. As businesses grew larger and more complex, so did the number and variety of their transactions. By the 15th century, traders required quite elaborate records to support their business, and in 1494 an Italian monk, Luca Pacioli, provided them with an ideal system in a pioneering work on double-entry book-keeping. This allowed them to record transactions and analyse them by type of revenue and expenses, as well as by class of assets and liabilities. Centuries later, the German poet Goethe would call it 'the finest invention of the human mind'; it remains the foundation of modern accounting.

THE GUILD SYSTEM

Many merchants were fairly unpopular. Renart le Contrefait, a 14th-century French satirist, for example, had a jaundiced view of the rising merchant class, particularly of the way they were prepared to finance

TABLEWARE
A 15th-century French or German silver-gilt drinking cup is typical of the tableware used in wealthy homes.

MONKEY BUSINESS People quite often kept monkeys as pets, as is seen in this 15th-century French jeweller's shop.

BOOK-KEEPING A merchant's clerk records all transactions before goods are collected for shipment.

The role of the guild was to maintain standards within a craft and to protect its members from competition. It controlled wages and prices, checked that no master took on more apprentices than he could manage, and set conditions and a scale of fees by which a journeyman could become a master.

Guilds were proud and powerful institutions, with expensive uniforms and liveries, as well as elaborate systems of professional etiquette. Each guild levied a weekly subscription from its members, creating a fund from which a member was provided with money if he became unemployed or sick, and from which pensions were paid to the widows of former members. The fund also paid for Masses to be said for the souls of dead members and for pageants on holy days.

Most guilds had their own inspectors, and some had their own police forces and jails to deal with troublesome workers. Wherever possible, the punishment was made to fit the crime. One wine merchant was convicted of selling adulterated wine in 14th-century London and was sentenced accordingly: 'The said John Penrose shall drink a draught of the same wine which he sold to the common people and the remainder of such wine shall then be poured on

wars without being actively engaged in the contest. 'They live in a noble manner,' he wrote, 'wear lordly garments, have falcons, sparrow hawks, fine palfreys and fine chargers. When the vassals must go to join the host, the burgesses rest in their beds; when the vassals go to be massacred in battle, the burgesses picnic by the river.'

'YOU MAY EITHER TAKE A NAP OR STROLL ABOUT'

❛ When you are in the market town be polite and agreeable; then you will secure the friendship of all good men. Make a habit to rise early in the morning, and go first and immediately to church ... If you are unacquainted with the traffic of the town, observe carefully how those who are reputed the best and most prominent merchants conduct their business. You must also be careful to examine the wares that you buy before the purchase is finally made to

make sure that they are sound and flawless ... call in a few trusty men to serve as witnesses as to how the bargain was made.

You should keep occupied with your business till breakfast or, if necessity demands it, till midday; after that you should eat your meal. After the meal you may either take a nap or stroll about a little while for pastime and to see what other good merchants are employed with, or whether any new wares have come to

the borough which you ought to buy.

Finally, remember this, that whenever you have an hour to spare you should give thought to your studies, especially to the law books ... and further, there are certain things which you must be aware of and shun like the devil himself; these are drinking, chess, harlots, quarrelling, and throwing dice for stakes. ❜

Anonymous advice to a 13th-century Norwegian merchant

AVARICE **Bankers are depicted as symbols of avarice in a 14th-century Italian treatise on the seven deadly sins.**

the head of the same John and he shall forswear the calling of vintner in the City of London forever.'

At times of recession, guild members would act together, all lowering wages at the same time, and refusing to employ any recalcitrant workers. Although, in the early days, membership of a guild was open to any master of the craft concerned, the poorer craftsmen were gradually squeezed out, and guilds became monopolistic syndicates of the rich.

A SPLASH OF COLOUR **A craftsman decorates a room. Many buildings, both inside and out, were brightly coloured and craftsmen were highly skilled.**

One of the many ways in which town life differed from country life, was in the organisation and behaviour of labour. Apart from moments of mass unrest, such as the rising of the Jacquerie in France in 1358 – it got its name from the French *jacques*, the popular term for a peasant – and the Peasants' Revolt in England in 1381, labourers in the country seldom offered any opposition to the orders of the lord of the manor. Either a peasant worked the land or he and his family starved.

In towns, however, things were different. Building workers regularly downed tools when their wages were in arrears – or for more bizarre reasons, as at Obazine in France in the 12th century, when a vegetarian abbot threw away the carcass of a pig that workers had killed and had been planning to eat for dinner. In 1339 carpenters in London were fined for intimidating foreign workers who were willing to work for less than the standard 'sixpence a day' and an after-dinner drink. Butchers and bakers frequently went on strike if they were not allowed to raise the price of meat or bread when supplies were scarce; the town councils usually retaliated at such times by lifting the ban on meat or bread being imported into town for resale. And in Florence in 1378, the lowest-paid workers, or *ciompi*, rebelled, demanding higher wages: '*Viva il popolo!*' they cried, in an early demonstration of class consciousness.

BED, BOARD AND DRINK

As the number of travellers grew, the old monastic hostelries
were replaced by increasingly luxurious inns and guest houses.

DINING OUT Guests at an inn are served a meal under the watchful eye of
the landlord in this 14th-century Italian illustration.

IN EARLY MEDIEVAL TIMES, the hardships travellers had to contend with outweighed the few compensatory comforts. Most European countries were still hunting-grounds for bears and wolves. The roads were poor, and there were plenty of robbers, thieves and outlaws lurking a short distance from the protective walls of the towns. Only the wealthy could afford the luxury of travelling on horseback and the security of an armed escort. For most travellers, journeys were on foot and painfully slow, 20 miles in a day being a great achievement.

But as trade increased, so did the demand for places of safety where traders could spend the night, while increasing numbers of pilgrims had similar needs. The first inns were generally Church foundations run by monks, where guests slept in long dormitories, with no fires and only simple fare – bread and a little cheese, perhaps, and water, mead or weak ale to drink. Occasionally travellers would find lodging in a local manor house and, as lords of the manor became wealthier and moved to bigger houses, some of the manor houses became inns.

The first European inns offered few luxuries, but guests could usually find better food, greater warmth and more convivial company than in the older monastic hostelries. Most inns consisted of a large hall, with storerooms and outbuildings to the side. Trestle tables were erected on the stone floor of the hall, and all the guests ate together, the food consisting of a roast dish, perhaps, or a stew of beans and bacon.

When the evening meal was over (few inns provided food at midday), the tables were removed, and the guests would curl up in their cloaks to sleep on the floor, sometimes on straw mattresses but more often on a few rushes strewn near the fire. The straw and rushes were riddled with fleas and lice, and scattered with scraps of old food, animal droppings and puddles of spilled wine and beer. In some inn yards there were troughs of water big enough to let people bathe, but few made use of this except in the height of summer.

Even so, there were still some surprising dangers for the unwary traveller. In the 12th century, John Jarman and his wife, who ran the Aegelward Inn at Colnbrook, then a day's journey from London, were convicted of the murder of a Reading clothier. The murder weapon was a bed, built over a trapdoor operated by a lever. When it fell, the bed tilted and the clothier was precipitated into a vat of boiling water below. The Jarmans confessed to 60 such murders; they had robbed the bodies for money and valuables, and had then claimed that their victims had left the inn without paying.

Later came greater comfort, better food, more privacy and even bed linen (although this was likely to be

BED AND BOARD Customers at a
German guest house enjoy a simple
meal together.

DOING THE SHOPPING Villagers gather for a chat as they are served with wine and bread, two staple ingredients in the daily diet. This Italian fresco is from the school of Domenico Ghirlandaio.

verminous). Many of the newer inns had separate rooms, often on an upstairs floor with a galleried corridor running along outside. Outbuildings included coal-holes, an oven-house and kitchen, and privies. The cost of food and shelter for the night in the 14th century was about 4 pence – a day's wages for most. Monastic inns were cheaper, charging a halfpenny for a bed and a farthing for candles for the night.

In rural areas, ale-kitchens were the forerunners of country inns – simply kitchens in private houses where villagers gathered to buy a jug of home-brewed ale. In England the ale was sweet, and flavoured with sage or honey; in France, Burgundy, the Low Countries and the Holy Roman Empire, the beer was brewed with hops, and was stronger and less sweet. Most countries passed laws to regulate the quality and quantity of the ale or beer provided.

These country beer-houses and ale-kitchens had poor reputations. An anonymous writer in the 14th century roundly condemned them: 'The tavern is a well of gluttony, for it may be called the devil's schoolhouse and the devil's chapel, for there his disciples stand and sing, both day and night, and there the devil doth miracles to his servants . . .' William Langland, in *Piers the Plowman*, listed the many customers found at the tables of a medieval inn: the shoemaker, the tinker and his apprentices, the needle-seller, the parson, the ditcher, the fiddler and the ratter, a rope-maker, a horse-hirer, a cobbler and a butcher.

There were no fixed hours of opening. An ale-house or tavern opened when it liked and served customers from sunrise until late at night. All of them, however, would be subject to any local curfews, and drunk or sober, few people wished to trudge home along dark roads.

THE CHURCH IN ACTION

'There is one holy catholic and apostolic church, outside of which there is neither

salvation nor remission of sins,' proclaimed Pope Boniface VIII in 1302 –

one of many constant reminders that the Church sought to control the life and destiny of all.

HE CHRISTIAN CHURCH lay so much at the heart of medieval life that, if you wanted to know how long to boil an egg, there were recipes which recommended 'the time wherein you can say a Miserere'. The calendar was a map of religious festivals and seasons: Lent, Advent, All Saints' Day, All Souls' Day, Michaelmas, Martinmas, Easter and the Nativity. Every Friday was a fast day by order of the Church; every Sunday a day for attending Mass. Holidays were holy days, days that commemorated the work or death of a saint, a victory for the soldiers of Christ, or some special event in the life of the Saviour or the Virgin Mary. People worked or went on pilgrimages, feasted or fasted, sang or were silent as the Church dictated.

The hold of the Church over people's lives lasted from the cradle to the grave – and beyond, into life everlasting. It was an age of miracles. Few years went by without reports of the work or suffering of some new saint, or some example of the power of God being witnessed by a poor shepherd or peasant girl.

To be excommunicated, or cast out of the Church and denied its sacraments, was the gravest of all punishments – for with excommunication came the certainty of eternal damnation.

It was the desire for salvation that kept the Church in power. Every Sunday, as they stood in humble village churches, private chapels or in the great cathedrals that were rising all over Europe, congregations were reminded of the choice that lay before them. Obey the teachings and dictates of the Church and live for ever with the Lord; disobey and writhe for eternity in hell fire. The paintings on church walls spoke more eloquently than any sermon of the tortures that awaited those who failed to render unto God that which was God's – down to the payment of religious tithes and taxes.

For those who needed help and advice to gain this salvation, there were plenty of representatives of the Church on hand. Proportionately, more people than ever before or since were paid servants of the Church. At the head was the Pope, Christ's Vicar on earth – or, for the latter part of the 14th century, two popes, one in Rome and the other in Avignon, the 'Babylon of the West', according to the Italian poet, Petrarch. The papacy had its own territory, army, diplomatic corps and bureaucrats dispensing – at a price – permits for a range of activities from receiving stolen goods to marrying a second cousin once removed.

Below the popes in religious ranking came a vast organisation of cardinals, archbishops, bishops, priors,

A CHURCH BELL-RINGER
A common sound of the Middle Ages was the chiming of bells, regulating times of prayer and work for everyone, from king to serf.

DID YOU KNOW?

A young pilgrim at Santo Domingo de la Calzada in northern Spain was falsely accused of theft, hanged, and his body left to rot on the gallows. After praying to St Dominic, however, his parents found that he was still alive. When this story was reported to the judge who had convicted the man, he dismissed it, saying that the roast chicken on the plate before him was as likely to come back to life. The chicken then miraculously flapped its wings and flopped off the judge's table. The young man's innocence was later proved.

To the Glory of God Masons prepare stones to be hoisted to the top of a Gothic cathedral by a treadmill crane, while unskilled journeymen mix the mortar.

abbots, prioresses, monks, nuns, friars, clerks, chaplains, priests and pardoners. Bishoprics and monasteries were among the greatest employers and landowners in medieval Europe. They had their own courts, police forces and prisons. The clergy had special privileges, one of the most useful of which was known as 'benefit of clergy'. This gave the right to anyone in holy orders to be tried by a church court, whatever the charge (when dealing with one of their own number, church courts naturally tended to pass lighter sentences than secular courts). The privilege was gradually extended to students and church-wardens, and then to all who could read – reading and writing being regarded almost as a church monopoly. Nevertheless, there were a great many priests who were unable to read, and could not understand the

91

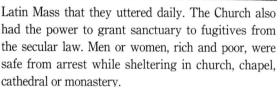

CHURCH DIGNITARIES The Archbishop of Rheims greets Charles V of France at the door of his cathedral in 1365. Chaucer's Prioress (above) rides with the Canterbury pilgrims.

Latin Mass that they uttered daily. The Church also had the power to grant sanctuary to fugitives from the secular law. Men or women, rich and poor, were safe from arrest while sheltering in church, chapel, cathedral or monastery.

The power and privileges of the Church were open to abuse, and throughout the Middle Ages criticism of the officers and teachings of the Church grew. John Wycliffe in England and Jan Huss in Bohemia preached an extreme version of the doctrine of pre-destination, which holds that man is preordained to salvation or damnation – regardless of the priesthood.

Unlike the monks, the friars – Franciscans, Dominicans, Carmelites and Augustinians – were expected to mix with the laity. Many of these travelling friars brought a new religious fervour to the towns and villages they visited. Others, like those portrayed in Boccaccio's *Decameron*, lived lives of ease, taking from the poor, and living off the fat of the land. In the words of a 14th-century English poem:

> *I have lived now 40 years,*
> *And fatter men about the ears,*
> *I never saw yet than these friars …*

The most serious criticisms were levelled at the pardoners, who raised money for the Church by selling absolution for every sin, from gluttony to murder. At the close of the Middle Ages, this debasement of the Church's power to save a man's soul provided much of the ammunition for Martin Luther and others in their attack on the Church.

Though the friars had a bad name, most people admired the life of quiet self-denial lived by medieval monks and their round-the-clock ritual of prayer. Monasteries and convents provided shelter and accommodation for travellers, and sanctuary and employment for ordinary people. Although most monastic orders would not accept illegitimate children, any man or woman who wished to renounce the world could enter as a novice, and then either stay as a lay brother or sister, or take vows and become a fully fledged member of the community.

At its best, the Church was a magnificent and idealistic institution: a centre of learning and knowledge; a provider for the poor, the sick and the dying; and a patron of science and the arts. For example, the Cistercian monks were the most advanced metallurgists, farmers and vintners in Europe, and the monastic orders in general knew more about medicine and healing than any medieval doctors, save the great Arab physicians.

Magnificent cathedrals and churches were commissioned by the Church; and the most beautiful

A Monk: from Matins to Vespers

BROTHER WALTER'S DAY began at midnight, or as near to midnight as could be calculated. Walter and nine or ten brother monks rose from their box beds in the monastery dormitory, a room lit by a single candle all night, robed, and made their way to the cloister outside the chapel. Here all the monks assembled and processed into chapel for Matins, the first service of the day. Latecomers had to prostrate themselves, stretching face down on the stone floor, to seek atonement before the sub-prior would allow them to take their places in the choir stall.

After Matins, Walter returned to bed until some time between five and six in the morning. Then it was back to chapel for Prime, a shorter service than Matins, followed by a breakfast of bread and ale. For some two hours, Walter and his brothers read quietly together in the cloisters, examining old texts and manuscripts that told the stories of the lives of the great saints. At nine o'clock there was a further service – Chapter Mass which all the monks attended and at which a Chapter of the Rule of the monastery was read aloud. The sub-prior listened to complaints about the monks' behaviour, and gave his verdict as to what should happen to those guilty of breaking the Rule.

At eleven o'clock High Mass was sung in the chapel. The praises of God echoed from the stone walls; the scent of incense rose to the arched

MONASTERY WINE
A cellarer helps himself to a drop.

roof; and rays of light poured into the chapel through the beautiful stained-glass windows.

After High Mass it was time for work. Each monk had his own set of tasks to perform – in the fields or the workshops, in the library or the kitchens, in dairy or brewery. Brother Walter, however, worked in the cloisters, copying illuminated manuscripts in Latin script.

At two o'clock the bell rang for dinner, and the other monks joined Brother Walter in the cloisters. After washing their hands they then processed once more into the refectory. Grace was sung by all the monks, who then sat in silence at the long wooden

tables, eating soup, bread, dishes of vegetables, eggs and a little cheese, and drinking ale brewed in the monastery. On feast days, meat and fish were also served. While Walter and his brother monks ate, one brother read to them from the Bible.

The monks had the afternoon off: for resting, reading or studying. Before the evening meal at six o'clock, however, they were expected to spend some time in prayer. After supper, Compline – the last service of the day – was sung in the chapel. Walter and his brothers then spent perhaps an hour or two talking quietly together in the gardens of the monastery in summer, or in the cloisters in winter. Those who tended the animals on the monastery farm made sure they were fed and secure for the night, and most monks retired early to the dormitory, knowing that the bell would ring at midnight for the start of another day.

OUTDOOR DEVOTIONS
A 15th-century monk preaches in the open air.

music was composed, played and sung to the glory of God. The Church was also the ladder by which people rose in society. The humble young man who learned to read and write, who became a holy clerk, and then took employment in the household of a bishop or archbishop, often advanced to a position of power and authority: there are many examples of medieval popes and cardinals from humble origins – for example, Pope Urban IV (1261–64), the son of a shoemaker, and Nicholas V (1447–55), the son of a poor physician.

THE CRUSADERS

Adventurers, criminals, priests and devoted followers of Christ –

the Crusaders included the best and worst of medieval society.

PREACHING WAR A 15th-century illustration shows Pope Urban II at the Council of Clermont, proposing a Christian Crusade against the infidels.

SELJUK TURKS defeated the armies of the Byzantine empire at the great battle of Manzikert in 1071 and, over the following 20 years, pushed them westwards as far as the Bosporus. Christian Europe was under attack – to such an extent that in 1095 at the Council of Clermont, Pope Urban II urged 'men of all ranks, knights and foot soldiers, rich and poor, to hurry to wipe out this evil race'. The Crusades were born. Over the next 200 years, thousands of bankrupts and booty-hunters, landless young nobles and wealthy warriors marched and sailed eastwards in the name of Christ whenever a Crusade was preached.

'I address thee fathers and sons and brothers and nephews,' declared one preacher in a Crusade sermon in 1098. 'If an outsider were to strike any of your own kin down would you not avenge your blood relative? How much more ought you to avenge your God, your father, your brother, whom you see reproached, banished from his estates, crucified; whom you hear calling, desolate and begging for aid.'

Most Crusaders financed their own expeditions and paid their own expenses – for a foot soldier, typically about £10 for an average campaign of three years. Going on Crusade ensured full remission for a person's sins – as well as more earthly dispensations, such as a moratorium on debt.

After the First Crusade captured Jerusalem in 1098, the city of Christ and the Holy Sepulchre became the goal of all Crusaders. In 1187, however, Muslim forces under the great Kurdish leader Saladin recaptured Jerusalem. Plagued by heat and flies, weighed down by chain mail, and bickering among them-

CRUSADERS' CASTLE
The concentric Krak des Chevaliers in the Lebanon is 2300 feet above sea level. It has round towers, rather than square ones, because they are better at deflecting missiles.

EMBARKATION A French illustration shows ships being loaded and provisioned, ready for departing Crusaders.

selves, the Crusaders failed in all subsequent attempts to retake the city. Of the tens of thousands of 10 to 14-year-olds who made up the Children's Crusade in 1212, for instance, two-thirds perished before they had even crossed the Alps, and most of the rest were sold into slavery once they reached the Mediterranean. The 'infidel' was never conquered, and continued to push westwards. In 1453 the Turks captured Constantinople, and by 1529 were at the gates of Vienna.

BATTLEFIELD MEETING
This illustration is thought to show the English King Richard (left) in mythical single combat with the Saracen leader Saladin.

Among the lasting everyday effects of the Crusades were a great increase in trade with the East, and a wealth of new ideas and goods. From the East came silk and muslin (from 'Muslim'), Persian and Turkish carpets, dried fruit, pomegranates, melons, lemons, perfumes, bath-houses, oils, rice, stirrups, wheel-

CLASH OF ARMS
Crusaders and Saracens fight it out in one 14th-century manuscript.

barrows; a revival of the art of glass-making and the laying of mosaic floors; Arabic numerals to replace Roman ones; and improvements in navigation and the design of ships.

THE ART OF WAR

'The dying roll about in the blood of strangers. The fallen bodies groan,

and the proud spirits moan horribly' – an eyewitness account of the Battle of Poitiers

captured the brutality of medieval warfare.

AR was a recurring plague on the Middle Ages. And even when neighbouring countries were officially at peace, there were frequent armed raids across frontiers – a couple of dozen men driving off cattle, firing a house or settlement, snatching what they could and killing those who got in their way. Armies of mercenary troops, sometimes numbering thousands of men, roamed Europe for much of the 14th and 15th centuries, exploiting the prevailing political instability to sell their services to the highest bidder.

People expected war; the nobles, in particular, lived for it; and everyone trained for it. A law passed by Edward III of England in 1365 forbade, on pain of death, all sport that took up time better spent in war training, especially archery practice. He also granted a moratorium on the debts of all workmen engaged in the making of longbows and arrows.

Of all European countries, France suffered the most. It was said that, as a result of the Hundred Years' War, there were children in France in the 15th century whose fathers, grandfathers, great-grandfathers and great-great-grandfathers had never known peace. Crops were destroyed, houses burnt, and towns and cities razed to the ground. Prices rose to ruinous levels. 'Every day and every night,' a Parisian recorded in his 14th-century journal, 'there were heard throughout Paris, because of the high prices, such long complaints, lamentations, sounds of sorrow and piteous cries … Night and day cried out men, women, little children, "Alas! I die of cold," or "of hunger".' People fought for food in the streets, eating what had been thrown out for the pigs. 'The wolves were so ravenous,' the author continued, 'that they unearthed with their claws the bodies of people buried in the villages and fields …'

Even more destructive than the wars themselves was the cost of war, which bankrupted whole economies – particularly as the feudal system, whereby a knight would provide so many soldiers to fight for so many days for his overlord, gradually gave way to a money economy. This meant that all soldiers were paid in cash and the war had to be financed by taxes and bank loans.

SIEGE WARFARE

There were far more sieges than pitched battles. A siege was under the control of an aggressor, as it could be lifted at any time, and a truce could be negotiated or a settlement made – luxuries that were harder to come by in battle. No commander would attempt an invasion without capturing or destroying the fortified positions of the enemy. Henry V's conquest of France at the beginning of the 15th century owed far more to his successful sieges than to his victory at Agincourt.

But sieges were expensive and time-consuming. No invader would attack a town, castle or fortress without first attempting to negotiate a settlement. Defenders of a besieged town knew that the mercenary troops in a besieger's army cost a great deal of money to keep in the field, and that troops raised by feudal levy were obliged to serve for only a

---

BATTLE BURNS

Defenders of a besieged castle seldom used boiling oil on attackers, but preferred to hurl rocks, scalding water or wine, or hot sand. Sand entered the crevices of an attacker's armour, causing severe burns or suffocation. At the siege of Caen in 1417, Sir Edmund Springhouse fell from a scaling ladder into the dry moat. The French defenders of the city threw burning straw on to him as he lay in the ditch unable to rise, and he was roasted alive in his armour.

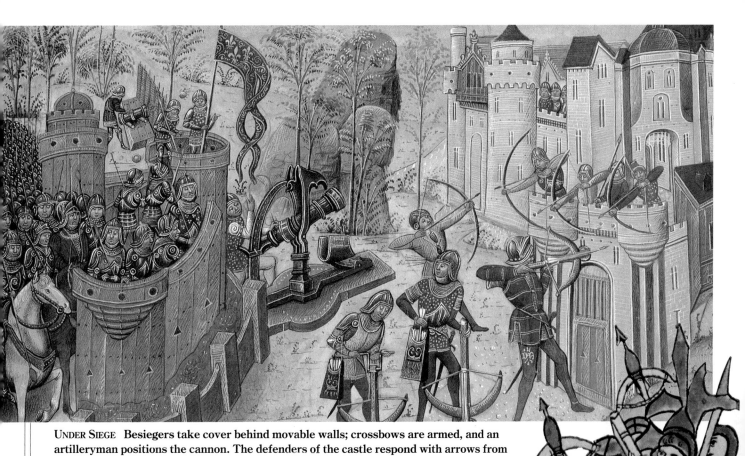

UNDER SIEGE Besiegers take cover behind movable walls; crossbows are armed, and an artilleryman positions the cannon. The defenders of the castle respond with arrows from their longbows. A group of crossbowmen (right) prepare to fire flaming arrows.

limited period – usually 40 days a year. Pressure was therefore as much on the attackers as the defenders to reach a peaceful agreement. Morale was important for both sides, too. The severed heads of enemy soldiers were lobbed by catapult into a castle or city to demoralise the defenders.

The chivalric code ruled that, if a besieged town or castle surrendered before hostilities began, the garrison and inhabitants should be allowed to march away unhindered – often keeping their weapons. Once a call to surrender had been refused, however, the besiegers were within their rights to slaughter all the inhabitants and burn the city to the ground. In 1133 King Alfonso of Aragon invited the citizens of Mequinenza to surrender, promising them safe-conduct and the right to take with them all their possessions. They refused. Three weeks later, Alfonso's troops captured an outpost of the town. The garrison sued for peace. Alfonso refused to negotiate, stormed the town and beheaded every man.

When a town or castle fell, there was often a complete breakdown in the discipline of the conquering army. In 1204, when Constantinople fell to the armies of the Fourth Crusade, the Doge of Venice and the other leaders of the Crusaders allowed their troops to sack the city.

It was said that fires destroyed 'more houses than stood in the three largest towns of France'. Christian monasteries, convents and churches were looted by Christian troops, and Santa Sophia was gutted. The altar screen was torn to pieces, paintings were destroyed, and the Crusaders placed a French prostitute on the patriarchal throne, where she sang bawdy songs through her nose, in imitation of Byzantine chant.

If a town could not be starved into submission, many weapons existed to push home a direct assault. The most destructive weapon was fire, especially in the summer or at harvest time when the streets were likely to be covered in straw or chaff. Fire arrows were made by winding 'tow' (fibres of flax or jute wound together to form a rough rope impregnated with pitch) round the shaft of an arrow. The tow was lit and the flaming arrow fired. Bombs were made by filling barrels, or terracotta or glass pots, with flaming pitch, tar or animal fat. Small fire bombs were thrown by hand; larger ones were catapulted into the besieged town or castle, and burst open on landing, spreading fire and fear among the defenders. Burning liquid was also shot from hand pumps – an early form of flamethrower. Some attackers used animals to haul burning ropes or bundles of rags into a town by way of the sewers.

The most destructive incendiary device was 'Greek fire', a 7th-century Byzantine invention brought to Europe by returning Crusaders. It was first used in the 12th century, at the sieges of Montreuil-Bellay in France and Nottingham in England. In 1280 Marcus Graecus included a recipe for Greek fire in his work, *The Book of Fires for the Burning of Enemies*. Sulphur, tartar, sarcocolla (a sticky gum-resin), pitch, boiled salt and oil were all boiled together. Tow was then steeped in this mixture, and ignited just before it was hurled against the enemy.

Gas was also used as a weapon. During the crusade against the Albigensian heretics in France in 1209, the defenders of one besieged stronghold lowered a sack of sulphur, tow and glowing embers

SIEGE WEAPON A 15th-century artilleryman fires his horse-drawn, muzzle-loading cannon.

onto groups of attackers at the base of the town walls. The sack burst into flames and the burning sulphur gave off choking fumes, which forced the attackers to retreat. Clay gas bombs were filled with burning sulphur, pitch, resin and horses' hoofs. At the siege of Carolstein in 1422, Prince Coribut, in the service of the Duke of Lithuania, had the bodies of his own dead soldiers catapulted into the town with 2000 cartloads of manure to spread disease among the defenders.

In prolonged sieges a variety of towers, platforms and catapults were built by both attackers and defenders. The belfry (or *beffroi*) was a tower on wheels, which was rolled or hauled by oxen towards

THE BATTLE OF AGINCOURT: OCTOBER 25, 1415

❛ The mounted French threw themselves upon the English archers, who had their sharp stakes fixed before them; but the ground was so soft that the said stakes fell. And the French all retreated excepting three men; to whom it unluckily happened that by their horses falling on the stakes they were thrown to the ground, among the archers and were immediately killed. The remainder, or the greater part of them, with all their horses, from fear of the arrows, retreated into the French advanced guard in which they caused great confusion, breaking and exposing it in many places, and caused them to retire to some new-sown ground; for their horses were so wounded by the arrows that they were unmanageable. And thus the advanced guard being thrown into disorder, the men-at-arms fell in great numbers and their horses took to flight behind the lines ... The English archers, perceiving this disorder of the advanced guard, quitted their stakes, threw their bows and arrows on the ground and seizing their swords, axes and other weapons, sallied out upon them, and hastening to the places where the fugitives had made breaches, killed and disabled the French ... ❜

From the writings of a 15th-century monk from St Rémy, France

STORMING A CASTLE Armoured figures scale ladders, while others (above) advance under a portable shelter, perhaps to mine the castle's foundations.

the walls of a besieged castle or city. The tower had several platforms, connected by ladders, and was used as a base from which archers could fire at defenders. Some belfries had hinged drawbridges which were lowered onto the castle wall, enabling the besiegers to storm the castle.

The primary function of the *trebuchet* or *mangonel* was as a giant catapult, hurling stones weighing up to 200 pounds distances of up to 300 yards. Worked by teams of men, the trebuchet had an astonishing rate of fire. At the siege of Lisbon in 1147, two such engines fired 5000 stones between them in a single day – a rate of one stone per engine every 30 seconds. When used with a counterweight (which sometimes weighed 15 tons), the trebuchet could also lift platforms of attackers to the parapet of a besieged castle.

The *ballista* was a giant crossbow, used as much by defenders as attackers. It shot large wooden arrows or bolts, iron-tipped and flecked with iron or

brass studs. The bolt had great penetration and could skewer several victims at a time. Before any direct assault, the walls had to be breached or the gates smashed open. Huge battering rams were constructed for this purpose, roofed over to protect the teams of up to 60 men who swung the ram. They were made of the largest available tree trunks, often fitted with a metal head. The bore was similar to a battering ram but was turned like a drill to eat away at the wall. When a section of wall was under attack from such machines, defenders would lower thick, padded mats stuffed with straw, hides or wool, to cushion the wall against the pounding.

Where walls were strong enough to withstand battering, they were undermined instead. Protected by movable sheds (called 'sows'), groups of miners approached the base of the wall and began digging under the foundations. As they dug, the tunnel was shored up with timber props and, once the miners had burrowed beneath the wall itself, the hole was filled with combustible material, which was then ignited. As the timber props burnt away, the sector of the wall collapsed. It took a lot of fuel for mining to succeed, however. At the siege of Rochester in 1215, King John

BOLTS OF FIRE The shafts of arrows and clubs were coated with flammable material and set alight just before they were fired.

THE WEAPONS OF WAR

HAND GUN The bracket on the barrel of this early musket was rested on a wall or other support to take the recoil.

APART FROM THE LONGBOW and the crossbow, the main infantry weapon was the pike. This was a long pole, tipped with a sharp metal head. It was used mostly as a defensive weapon, to halt charging enemy cavalry. Rows of pikemen stood in line, the butt ends of their pikes firmly pushed into the ground, with the heads pointing roughly at the level of a horse's head, like a hedge of thorns. Pikes were much longer than cavalry lances (Swiss pikes – the best – were over 18 feet long).

Each country had its own preferred weapon for other foot soldiers. The Flemings favoured the mace – an

READY FOR COMBAT Heavy suits of armour such as this were in use from about 1200. Knights' weapons included maces and halberds (above). They wielded massive swords (right) capable of piercing their opponents' armour.

CANNON'S MOUTH
This early 'bombard' was made from strips of iron, bound together with iron hoops.

enormous club, sometimes studded with iron spikes. The Swiss, who were the finest infantry troops of the Middle Ages, preferred the halberd, a long-handled axe with a spearhead projecting beyond the axe blade.

Each knight and foot soldier also carried a small dagger for hand-to-hand fighting. Not until the end of the 15th century were small 'hand gonnes' developed, and at no time during the Middle Ages were they as effective as longbows and

crossbows. At the beginning of the Middle Ages, most knights were protected by the hauberk, a long coat of chain mail covering the entire body from neck to feet, leaving only the head and hands uncovered.

The trouble with chain mail was that it provided a good defence only against the slash or cut of a sword. It was vulnerable, however, to a thrust from a sword, pike or lance, and was easily penetrated by an arrowhead. By the 14th century chain mail had been almost entirely replaced by plate armour.

A complete set of plate armour weighed some 70 pounds and was a wonder of articulated engineering. The only problem was insufficient ventilation, and many knights suffocated in the heat of battle.

BATTLE DRESS An armourer makes a mail shirt, a piece of equipment that hardly changed in 500 years.

THE HUNDRED YEARS' WAR The English and French fleets clash at the Battle of Sluys off the Flemish coast in 1340.

wrote to Hubert de Burgh, demanding animal fat to feed the fires in the mines his men had dug: 'We command you that with all haste, by day and by night, you send us 40 bacon pigs of the fattest and least good for eating, to bring fire under the tower ...'

The only defence against mining was either to build upon rock, or to countermine, breaking into the shaft and killing the attackers, or flooding the mine. Flooding, however, was not often an option, as defenders were unlikely to have sufficient water.

THE CHANGING FACE OF BATTLE

On the battlefield – as opposed to the siege – the knight, armed with sword and lance, was the most powerful and effective warrior in the early Middle Ages. Mounted on large warhorses, ten knights were said to be worth at least 100 foot soldiers, who showed little resistance to a cavalry attack. Indeed, during the 12th century, infantry was used simply to absorb the shock of enemy cavalry attacks so that their own cavalry could assess the strength of the enemy and prepare a counterattack.

This changed with the development of the crossbow and, more so, with the longbow. By the end of the 12th century, bows were powerful enough to fire an arrow that could pierce 4 inches of oak. There is one documented case of an arrow fired from an elm longbow by a Welsh archer which nailed a knight to his horse; it went through the flap of the knight's chain-mail shirt, through his mail breeches, his thigh and his wooden saddle, and then penetrated the flank of his horse.

The best longbows were cut from yew or ash and were custom-made to suit the weight and size of the

101

men using them. Longbow arrows had an effective range of at least 200 yards, and an experienced archer could loose between ten and twelve arrows per minute. A crossbow took longer to operate, for the bolt had to be pulled back by a winding mechanism – two bolts per minute was the maximum rate of fire – and it was not until the end of the 14th century that the crossbow achieved anything like the range and penetrative power of the longbow.

Gunpowder and artillery played little part in siege warfare before the 15th century, although cannon were used as early as the siege of Metz in 1324. Early cannon were called 'bombards' (from the Greek *bombos*, a loud hum). At first they were made of copper or brass, and were fitted with removable breeches for loading cannonballs of oak (with iron casings) or lead. 'The bombard made such a noise in the going as though all the devils of hell had been in the way,' wrote one contemporary. These primitive bombards were soon replaced by muzzle-loading iron cannon, however. Iron sheets were forged into tubes bound together by hoops that were heat-shrunk over them. Stone cannonballs replaced metal. Large cannon weighed up to 10,000 pounds, and could hurl a ball weighing 1000 pounds several hundred yards.

By the end of the Middle Ages, artillery had completely changed the art of warfare. The supremacy of the English longbow on the battlefield was shattered once French artillery came into action

NO QUARTER **Most cities had their own armed troops. In Paris (above) militiamen slaughter invaders. An archer (left) strings his longbow.**

in the 15th century. Few castles could withstand the pounding of cannonballs. The outcome of sea battles was no longer settled by grappling, boarding and hand-to-hand fighting. Soon the cannon was to be found in almost every European army. The Italian poet, diplomat and scholar, Petrarch, recorded its rapid rise to supremacy: 'so quick and ingenious are the minds of men in learning the most pernicious arts,' he commented sadly.

RAISING AN ARMY

Since England had no standing army, skilled soldiers made themselves available for private hire – at wages superior to those of skilled craftsmen. Throughout Europe the more important towns kept their own bands of militia, on a more or less permanent footing. Paris maintained a contingent of crossbowmen called the Corporation des Arbalatiers; Rouen had a defence force of 60 men-at-arms and 180 archers; and Calais had a local army of 1000 men. These militia groups had several functions – not only to defend the town from attack by outlaws or marauders, mercenaries or foreign troops, but also to keep order by patrolling unruly quarters, and to protect the town's independence from royal aggression.

FIRE POWER

Medieval gunpowder was composed of 41 per cent saltpetre, 29.5 per cent sulphur and 29.5 per cent charcoal made from hazel twigs (modern proportions are 75 per cent saltpetre, 10 per cent sulphur and 15 per cent charcoal). It was unrefined and inefficient – much of the power of the blast was wasted in fires which raged within the mouth of the cannon long after the shot had been fired. It was also expensive, costing six times the price of lead, and 25 times that of iron.

Knights, archers and artillerymen were all warriors with special skills: the common soldier had none. With few exceptions he was as much despised and distrusted by his own leaders as by the enemy. Most foot soldiers wore ordinary clothes in battle, reinforced with leather patches and strips of metal or quilted cloth. The better-equipped had iron skullcaps, thick leather jerkins and any pieces of armour that they had been able to collect for themselves while campaigning. They were on the whole a ragged-looking lot, with no *esprit de corps*, or sense of common bonding such as was shared by the superbly equipped knights.

THE COMMON SOLDIER

One Flemish knight was scathing in his opinion of his own foot soldiers, who were regarded by many as among the best in Europe: 'These churls think of nothing but evil. I know a good fate for them: they should be dragged off and hanged. Their beard is too long; they cannot escape, they are good for nothing except under restraint.'

Not surprisingly, the common soldier often felt inferior. Yet it took only one victory for his morale to soar. At Courtrai in 1302, one Flemish infantryman with his *goedendag* (mace) took on two mounted French knights in combat. And after Bannockburn in 1314, Thomas Grey of Heaton recorded that 'the Scots have become so courageous and spirited that they conquer the Border countries, and the English dare not wait for them. Such is their superiority that they scarcely give the enemy a thought.'

Pay for the common soldier varied, both in amount and regularity. A soldier received anything from two to eight pence a day for between 40 and 90 days' service a year – at a time when land could be rented for four pence per acre per year. In times of need, leaders were prepared to offer more – King John paid two shillings a day per man for mercenaries early in the 13th century. When food was available, the common soldier ate considerably better than the peasant. His main diet consisted of rye bread, peas, beans, fish, cheese, olive oil, a little butter, salt, vinegar, onions and garlic, and there was usually

---

EYEWITNESS

'LET NOTHING REMAIN ANYWHERE'

CIVIL WAR rent England for several years during the reign of King Stephen (1135–54) – between the forces of the King and of his cousin Matilda, a rival (and more legitimate) claimant to the throne. This passage describes one of Stephen's campaigns in the West of England:

❝ At last it seemed to King Stephen judicious to attack the enemy everywhere, plunder and destroy all that was in their possession, set fire to the crops and every other means of supporting human life and let nothing remain anywhere, that under this duress, reduced to the extremity of want, they might be at last compelled to yield and surrender. It was indeed

TERRORISM A woman protests as marauding bands set fire to peasant homes in 14th-century France.

evil, he thought, to take away the sustenance of human life that God had vouchsafed, yet far worse for the kingdom to be constantly disturbed

by the enemy's raiding and impoverished by daily pillage ... So gathering together a large body of finely equipped knights, his son too with his men and some of the barons massed on the opposite flank, he sets himself to lay waste that fair and delightful district, so full of all good things, round Salisbury; they took and plundered everything they came upon, set fire to houses and churches, and what was a more cruel and brutal sight, fired the crops that had been reaped and stacked all over the fields, consumed and brought to nothing everything edible they found. ❞

May 1149: *The Deeds of Stephen*, by an anonymous chronicler

plenty of poultry to be snatched from farms on the way. On active service a soldier received wine on feast days or on the eve of battle, but for the most part he drank ale, beer or cider. A wounded soldier received special privileges, with sugar, mustard and honey augmenting his diet.

Most contemporary records grossly exaggerate the number of soldiers employed. The chronicler Fulcher

ON THE MARCH A Bible illustration from the mid-13th century shows soldiers with their supplies and equipment.

A Mercenary in 14th-Century Europe

Aimerigot stretched his bruised limbs and gazed red-eyed into the grey dawn over the north Italian plain. It had been a good campaign – a long march from France, admittedly, but plenty of plunder on the way. The mercenaries had helped themselves to silks and furs, spices and gold from the wagon trains of the merchants they had met on the way. And what they had stolen they had sold at every town they passed through, to brokers who asked no questions and paid a good price – once they had seen the strength of the mercenaries.

Aimerigot and his comrades had eaten well off the country, for the peasants of the Auvergne, Provence and Lombardy had been persuaded – often at the point of a sword – to supply them with wheat and flour, fresh bread, hay for the horses, good wine, beef and mutton, fat lambs and poultry.

'When we ride forth,' thought Aimerigot, as he drained his breakfast cup of wine, 'we're provisioned like kings, and the country trembles before us.'

Yesterday's battle had been hard and bloody, but few towns could put troops into the field to match the disciplined fury of the White Company, breastplates and helmets gleaming in the sun, and the points of their spears and arrow tips sharper than the fangs of ravening wolves. This commander they had – Sir John Hawkwood – was reckoned the best general and tactician in Europe. So the town had fallen and neither church, house, inn nor merchant's storeroom had

After Agincourt
Soldiers share loot from fallen friends and foes.

been spared. In the rage that always followed a battle, there had been mortal sin committed, but so what? Aimerigot trusted his commander to negotiate a general absolution from the Pope for the mercenaries. It had been done plenty of times already. As one of Aimerigot's English comrades had said: 'If God Himself were a soldier, He would be a robber.'

of Chartres estimated that 600,000 troops set off on the First Crusade (1095–99) – the real number was probably between 12,000 and 20,000. Edward I had only 2500 troops when he invaded Wales in 1277. And Henry V commanded fewer than 6000 at the Battle of Agincourt. Armies, however, could generally be reckoned in hundreds, though they were often accompanied by servants and camp followers; for example, when the Duke of Alba invaded Flanders in the 16th century he took 400 courtesans with him.

THE DAY OF BATTLE

As soon as dawn broke, men were called to arms by trumpet calls. Tents were struck, huts dismantled and the overnight camp was broken. Men armed themselves before attending Mass, often taking Communion and making confession. Before the battle most soldiers were restless, and many were drunk.

Once the battle lines had been formed, leaders and commanders rode up and down, exhorting their men to do their best in the hours that lay ahead. John of Renesse gave detailed instructions to his Flemish troops before the Battle of Courtrai in 1302: 'Do not allow the enemy to break through your ranks. Do not be afraid. Kill both men and horses. "The Lion of Flanders" is our battle cry. When the enemy attacks the corps of Lord Guy, we shall come to your help from behind. Anyone who breaks into your ranks, or gets through, will be killed.'

The battle lines were closely packed ranks of men, standing shoulder to shoulder – with the exception of the mace men of Flanders, who needed space in which to swing their weapons. The atmosphere among the ranks was tense and nervous, for defeat meant ruin. Many of the soldiers would have been exhausted from long marches – perhaps 200 miles in 12 days – and would have been suffering from dysentery.

Most battles began with a cavalry charge, to probe weaknesses in the enemy's position. Like the infantry, the cavalry was packed tightly together. At a trot cavalry covered 250 yards a minute (around 9 miles per hour), but they charged at twice that speed. Archers covering the pikemen who waited to receive the cavalry charge had only some 15 to 25 seconds in which to shoot – little time to establish the closing range or to fire more than five arrows. But the archers were numerous, and thousands of arrows rained down on the cavalry from a height of some 100 feet.

As the cavalry crashed into the rows of pikemen, trumpets blew to encourage both armies. Horses reared up as they thundered onto the heads of the pikes, whinnying and screaming in terror. Knights roared their battle cries, both to terrify their opponents and to bolster their own courage. The noise was hellish. 'Drums and trumpets boom, if you are not used to these things you would soon be frightened,' wrote Guiart, a French foot soldier of the 13th century, on campaign in Flanders. 'Four hundred carpenters would not make such noise. They closed in with such force that the clash of weapons and the din of blows made the air ring, just as though trees in the forest were being cut down with innumerable axes … The fighters were like woodcutters, chopping down the trees of a forest … The din was so frightful that one could not have heard even God's thunder … It was as if all the smiths in Brussels and Bruges were striking their anvils.'

SURRENDER Delegates from a 15th-century city deliver the keys to their victorious besiegers.

From that first charge there would be no let up in the fighting. Men saw their comrades fall, trampled under foot by the warhorses, stabbed and slashed where they lay. They saw others lifted from the ground on the points of the lances of the knights. They heard the screams of the wounded and the dying. The ground was splattered with blood. Fear and rage filled both sides with the adrenalin needed to maintain the fight, for weapons were heavy.

If the pikemen successfully withstood the cavalry charge, the order was given 'Foot soldiers, stand back!', and their ranks opened to permit the counter-charge by their own horsemen. As the rival mounted troops clashed, hand-to-hand fighting broke out – desperate work at close range with sword and shield, where fighters locked in combat were always in danger of a stab in the back from a third party. The battle lurched to and fro, both sides hurling their reserve troops forward to break the enemy's resistance. As order broke down, troops headed for the nearest rallying point – a banner, or a large cross carried by a priest. The Italians went into battle with a *carroccio*, a wagon with a banner on a tall pole and a vessel containing the consecrated Host. If the troops were scattered, they would regroup at the rallying point, dragging their wounded with them.

As the slaughter increased to a horrifying level, neither man nor horse was spared. If the ground was hard, a fall from his horse could well shatter the limbs of a knight; if the ground was wet, there was the danger of a wounded man drowning where he lay.

Some battles were over in less than an hour, but this was rare. In most cases, after hours of fighting, one side broke; it wavered at first, seeking to cover the withdrawal of baggage and supply trains, but steadily it lost ground until the moment of defeat arrived. Then the victors pressed their advantage and the vanquished fled from the field, knights being the first to flee; and the pursuit became frenzied and merciless, often maintained over several miles. The defeated fled to the nearest place of safety, a town or a castle, where those who were not too shaken to eat bartered what equipment they had left for bread and wine.

The chivalric code permitted the burning of harvests and villages by a conquering army; and soldiers could take any livestock. It was this prospect of loot and ransoms – probably more than anything else – that motivated the medieval warrior.

SIEGE OF RHODES Turkish troops dig trenches during a siege of the Crusader fortress in the 15th century.

Losses on both sides could be severe. The victors could expect to lose up to 50 per cent of their force, the vanquished even more. First aid was unknown and people generally recovered only from the lightest of wounds or if they were unusually resilient. Many died painful deaths from septic wounds or peritonitis during the days and even weeks following a battle. Those who survived fell to their knees to pray, before burying their dead.

MAPPING THE WORLD

Early maps were unreliable and fanciful, but as travellers revealed

unknown areas of the world, maps became more accurate.

WORLD VIEW A map by the Italian cartographer Fra Mauro in the late 14th century shows Europe, Africa and Asia as they were then thought to be.

MEDIEVAL TRAVELLERS had little access to maps. For journeys of any length, they used guides identifying routes by landmarks such as rivers, villages and hills. Between the age of the Egyptian geographer Ptolemy in the 1st century AD and the 12th century, map-making made little progress: indeed, copies of famous maps devised by Ptolemy were published as late as 1477 in Bologna and 1482 in Ulm. In 1492 Columbus was still using Ptolemy's calculations for the size of the earth when he set out across the Atlantic in

search of Asia – hence some of his confusion about the New World that he reached.

Map-making was dominated by a strictly Christian view of the world. Maps had to conform to the shape of the world specified by the Bible. In the early 6th century, Constantine of Antioch had defined a 'Christian topography', which depicted the earth

MEDITERRANEAN COAST A 14th-century Portolan chart of the western Mediterranean has the east at the top.

as a flat disc – a regressive step scientifically, since Ptolemy held that the earth was round. For several hundred years the finest maps were made by Arab cartographers, such as Ibn Haukal, whose *Book of Ways and Provinces* was published in the 12th century, and al Idrisi, who compiled a world map for the Christian King Roger of Sicily in 1154. The Arabs had adopted the compass long before the Europeans; these early compasses consisted of magnetised iron needles mounted on pivots in round wooden boxes. Only in the 15th century did cartographers discover that such needles did not point to true north, but at an angle from it that varied from place to place. Once this difference had been appreciated, and an allowance made, navigation became a far more precise art.

For much of the Middle Ages, maps were drawn with east rather than north at the top (hence the word 'orientation'), and with Jerusalem at the centre, in accordance with a ruling of the Church. These early maps were, among other things, extremely erratic in scale. An early example

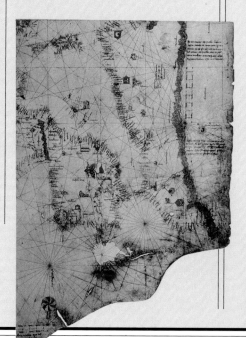

MISLEADING CALCULATIONS
Ptolemy calculates distances round the globe. Right: A Ptolemaic map from the 15th century. Below: A 13th-century astrolabe.

was the Peutinger Table (from the Roman word for map, *tabula*), copied from a Roman original in 1230, which represented the known world, from south-west Britain to the Ganges. Fifty years later came the *Mappae mundi*, circular maps depicting Europe, Africa and Asia. In 1250, Matthew Paris published the first notable map of England, based on Ptolemy's work, with north placed at the top. His map was hand-coloured, with green seas and blue rivers. Although objects of great beauty, such maps were of little practical use.

Far commoner and more useful were the Portolan charts made by seamen from Portugal, Catalonia and Italy in the years between 1300 and 1600. Pieced together from local surveys, these depicted the Mediterranean, and most of the European and African coastlines in bright colours on parchment made from the skin of sheep, goats or calves. The scale of these charts was often determined by the natural shape of the parchment – the largest measuring some 3 feet by 2 feet. Some were illustrated with pictures of fishes, emperors, castles and ships and, although they showed few if any inland details, islands and river deltas were sometimes gilded. Maps like these were much in demand at trade centres such as Genoa, Venice, Pisa and Barcelona. By the late 14th century, information from many Portolan charts had been pieced together to produce world maps, such as the Catalan map of 1375 and the magnificent world map of Fra Mauro of Murano, which was sufficiently up to date to incorporate the results of Marco Polo's travels and discoveries in the Far East.

One of the last great reproductions of the world before Columbus's travels in the Americas was the globe of Martin Behaim of Nuremberg: his 'earth apple' published in 1492. Within a few years, maps showing the discoveries of Columbus were being engraved and printed in Portugal, Spain, the Holy Roman Empire, France and Italy. Columbus, together with the Crusaders, pilgrims, soldiers, traders and sailors of the Middle Ages, had all played their parts in mapping the world.

In 1493, one commentator, Peter Martyr, paid fitting tribute to the pioneers: 'These wondrous men who have travelled across an unknown and boundless sea have taught us that there is nothing impossible for man.'

ALL-ROUND APPROACH
The globe or 'earth apple' was produced by a German cosmographer, Martin Behaim of Nuremberg.

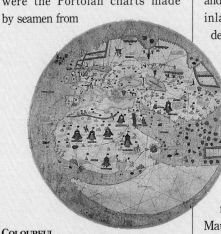

COLOURFUL WORLD The Catalan world map, decorated with emperors and local inhabitants.

ENFORCING LAW AND ORDER

Justice was rough and ready, punishment swift and merciless – the medieval miscreant was

seldom given time to reflect on his crime. Torture extracted confessions; branding, whipping and

mutilation were light sentences; execution was the frequent and ultimate deterrent.

HROUGHOUT FEUDAL EUROPE, the law was an irregular instrument, erratically applied. In theory the king or emperor was in charge – formulating laws, appointing judges and regulating punishments. But justice was rough, and the fate of any wrongdoer lay far more in the hands of the local lord. No country in Europe had a police force – it was the duty of everyone to pursue and apprehend criminals when the hue and cry was raised. It is hardly surprising, then, that crime was rife – and murder some 20 times as common per head of the population in 13th-century England as it is today.

TRIAL BY ORDEAL AND COMBAT

Most countries in the early Middle Ages had some system of trial by ordeal, whereby the accused's guilt or innocence was judged by the way the body reacted to intense heat. In Scandinavia, France and Germany, for example, the accused had to walk nine paces with bare feet over nine red-hot ploughshares – 'if he falters, if he does not press one of the ploughshares fully with his feet, if he is harmed the one least bit, then let him be judged guilty.' In England, the accused had to grasp a piece of red-hot iron, walk three paces with it and put it down. His hand was then bandaged and 'sealed', so that no treatment could be administered. After three days, the bandage was removed and the hand inspected; if the hand was healing without discoloration or suppuration, then the accused was pronounced innocent.

Alternatively, the accused could elect to prove his innocence in single combat with his accuser. In later years, accused and accuser could select champions to represent them. In 1152, the monks of St Germain-des-Prés selected a champion when an abbey serf was accused of trespass. 'The champions fought bravely: the St Germain man tore out his opponent's eye, felled him to earth, and compelled him to confess defeat, in virtue whereof the rights of the abbey were proclaimed.' Both methods were brutal ways of settling disputes, and by the 13th century they had

---

A COURT IN ACTION

THE FOLLOWING EXTRACTS are from court records at Holkham Manor in Norfolk. They date from 1332.

A fine of just one penny was fairly substantial. It would have been the equivalent of half a day's wages for most of the defendants.

❛ Thomas son of William drew blood from Bartholomew Cottyng spitefully and is fined 3d.

Bertha atte Drove broke into the house of Alice Digge and is fined 2d.

Margaret and Alice Otes broke the lord's pound for 4 pigs taken for a debt of the lord and for execution of the court's decisions. Fine 6d.

Agnes Bulwere rescued from the lord's bailiff a cow taken in the complaint of Alice Otes. Fine 3d.

John le Wrighte, Andrew Underclynt, Brother Adam of Derham, Edmund Haldeyn, John Silke, John Speller and Adam Crask made an illegal path over the land of Andrew Underclynt at the Clynt. Fine 1d each.

Court of Richard Neel, Henry Burgeys, Gilbert Burgeys and William de Waterden held on a Friday after the feasts of SS Peter and Paul. ❜

LAW BOOK This 13th-century book on English law observes: 'Two things are necessary for a king who rules rightly, arms and laws.' A monk and a nun in the stocks have been condemned to die by starvation.

fallen into disrepute – to be replaced by trial by jury. By the 15th century, the right to a jury was seen as one of the glories of English law. 'I would prefer 20 guilty men to escape,' wrote Sir John Fortescue, 'than one innocent to be condemned unjustly.'

TRIAL BY JURY

There were four pleas open to the accused: guilty, not guilty, pardon or benefit of clergy. A plea of pardon required evidence of some good deed done or some special service rendered to lord or country, meriting acquittal or a light sentence. What was termed 'Benefit of clergy' was granted only to those in holy orders, including novice monks, but was later extended to all who could read. The accused would then be tried in a church court, where the death penalty was not available. The few hardy souls who refused to plead were subjected to the torture known as *peine forte et dure* – the body being pressed with heavy weights until the accused died or capitulated.

The accused could represent himself or appoint someone to speak for him, and was tried before 12 or more jurors who were not there only to rule on the facts presented but also to produce evidence. The jurors were selected because they had been present when the crime had been committed. Their role, therefore, was not merely to deliver a verdict, but to amend the charge if they thought it wrong, to find one person not guilty and accuse another, and to give character references for the accused – since they usually came from the same town or village.

ESCAPE FROM THE TOWER

The first prisoner to escape from the Tower of London was Ranulf Flambard, Bishop of Durham, who had been imprisoned for refusing to accept a lay court's jurisdiction over his bishopric. In the Tower he was granted the right to send out for food and drink. On the night of February 2, 1106, he wined and dined his guards to the point of stupefaction, took a rope which had been hidden in a wine jar, tied it to the bars of his cell window and lowered himself to the ground 60 feet below. His servants were waiting for him, and took him to a boat on the Thames. Flambard reached France and safety.

Prison sentences were almost unknown, mainly because of the cost involved. Criminals, it was reckoned, should be a source of revenue rather than expense. A prison was simply a place for those awaiting trial or execution (usually two or three days after sentencing).

The village 'thieves' hole' was a small wooden hut with an earthen floor and a narrow opening in the door through which food could be passed if the prisoner was lucky. A sizeable town might have one or two prisons, but escapes were commonplace. Most gaolers were unpaid, and many purchased their position in expectation of fees and bribes from the prisoners. The worst places of confinement were 'pit prisons', found in most castles. Rather than prison, the priority in medieval times was to provide compensation. Fines were common, and usually coupled with a demand that the guilty promise to behave in future. Fixed fines were as low as a few pence for petty misdemeanours, but could be as high as £60 or £70 in late-medieval England for 'beating a knight'.

PUNISHMENTS TO FIT THE CRIME

Any fine was, of course, in addition to whatever capital or corporal punishment was decreed. Convicted thieves were often hanged; however, if the amount stolen was less than 12 pence in value (two or three days' wages for a labourer), or if the thief was

A DAY IN THE LIFE OF

A SHERIFF: THE POLICEMAN OF THE MIDDLE AGES

GUY DE GLYMPTON was conscious of his duties as Sheriff: 'to diligently make Inquiries upon the Articles touching the Crown and Dignity of our Lord the King'.

That meant dealing with a host of malefactors: 'Traitors, Thieves, Manslayers, Robbers, Murderers, Burners ... Mascherers (that sell and buy stolen meat knowing the same to be stolen) ... Redubbers of stolen cloths, that turn them into a new shape, and change the old one ... Outlaws ... Ravishers of Maids, Nuns and Matrons of good repute ... Usurers ... Takers of pigeons flying from Dovecotes ... them that shear Sheep by Night in Folds' — the list was almost endless.

Sheriff Guy was conscious that, although he had been appointed to collect the crown's rents and dues owed to the king, and to safeguard the king's interests in his shire of central England, he owed his appointment to the patronage of Walter de Niort, the most powerful local nobleman, whose views were often at odds with those of the king. The appointment cost Guy a considerable sum of money – well over £500, and it would be some time before the third of the profits from the shire court due to him reached that amount. Most of the court's takings would go to Walter – a fine from every offender, a fee from litigants who came to an agreement outside court, all the chattels of a condemned felon, and a fee from all those who wished to search the court rolls for information about the various dues or services they owed.

The day's work began. First, Guy checked the tithings – the list of all able-bodied men between 15 and 60 years old who would have to serve their turn in policing the shire and making it secure, and who would be called out to restore order in the event of an uprising. Then he inspected the prisoners awaiting trial. This gave him the opportunity to see how well Martyn the gaoler was performing his duties. Guy had sold Martyn the office of gaoler six months ago, when the shire court had last met.

But the bulk of the first day of the court would be taken up in collecting the rents due to the king. There would be the usual hand-wringing excuses and pleas for a smaller levy, and 100 or more good reasons why it was impossible to raise the money.

Guy smiled grimly to himself – since he was entitled to one-third of the profits from the court, he would insist on full payment, but take no more than was his due. Many of his fellow sheriffs had been found guilty of malpractice and had been dismissed. Doubtless Walter de Niort would have something to say on this subject.

prisoner was torn from the beam so that his ears were slit open, thus marking him for life. (Nose slitting was a common punishment for prostitutes.) The pillory was the favoured punishment for those selling adulterated or shoddy goods, or for tradespeople who had given their customers short measure. It was also the punishment commonly given to vagrants and vagabonds, or those who collected money under the false pretence that they were hermits or holy men.

TORTURE AND EXECUTION

Every country had its preferred methods of torture, as part of a punishment or to extract a confession. Prisoners were stretched on the rack – arms extended above their heads and ropes fastened to their wrists and ankles. The ropes were then steadily pulled in opposite directions, drawing both arms and legs from their sockets. A similar torture was to have the head stretched from the body by means of cords round the neck, under the chin. Thumbscrews were commonly used, or iron shoes which slowly crushed the victim's feet. Finger nails were torn out with pincers. The tongue was cut out, or a hole driven through it. Scolds and slanderers were subjected to the bridle, an iron helmet with spikes that entered the mouth, making speech impossible. Forgers and pickpockets might have their hands cut off.

Most executions were held in public and a holiday atmosphere prevailed, with itinerant salesmen selling

JUSTICE AT WORK
Judges sit at one end of Westminster Hall; clerks keep records, and the accused, in chains, await their trial. Adulterers (right) are led naked through the town.

cakes and pies, fruits and sweetmeats. The axe was usually reserved for those of noble birth: the rope for the lower classes. In a cruel and sadistic age, there were those who refined methods of execution. When James I of Scotland was murdered in 1437, his mistress – Lady Joan Beaufort, the 'milk white dove' – invented suitable fates for his murderers. Sir Robert Graham, leader of the conspiracy, was nailed by the right hand to a gallows set on a cart and then dragged through the streets of Edinburgh. At the place of execution, hot iron spikes were driven into his arms and thighs, and his son was

less than 12 years old, a lesser punishment would be substituted. They might be branded or have their ears cropped. They might be whipped or placed in a pillory at the town 'cross'. The prisoner either sat on a low bench or on the ground, with his legs fastened through two holes in a hinged plank of wood, or he stood with his head and hands similarly fastened. It was usual to nail the ears of the prisoner to a cross beam. When the sentence had been served, the

113

A JUDGE: THE LEGAL SYSTEM AT WORK

WILLIAM OF PATTISHALL walked in stately procession to the Court of Assize. After the lawlessness that had followed the Peasants' Uprising a few years ago, it was important that the law reassert its authority.

The procession reached the courtroom. As he walked to his seat, William held himself proudly. He was a wealthy landowner, with a horse and a chest of woollen clothing as a gift from the king, and a chest of fine linen clothing from the queen. The week ahead could well be profitable – for he would be paid 24 pence each time he was called upon to explain the law, and would receive four pence from the successful party in each case. At the same time, William was conscious that he had to perform his duties fairly and honourably.

At the end of his year's training he had sworn an oath on holy relics that he would never knowingly misjudge a case. And, if any could prove him guilty of deliberate misjudgment, William knew that he would lose his office. The sheriffs had made the mistake of abusing their powers and had lost them. That was why William's office of justice had been created.

The hearings began. It was the usual parade of petty crime – poaching, fighting, stealing – and one more serious matter. A local tanner was accused of killing a labourer during a brawl outside a tavern. The accuser was the victim's brother, who had witnessed the slaying. The tanner, however, claimed that he had acted in self-defence. For William, the initial problem was to decide which of the two statements was to be tested by the court – that of the tanner or that of the victim's brother.

The jurors, several of whom had been eye-witnesses to the event, thought little of the tanner's explanation, and decided that was where the burden of proof should lie. The case ended two hours later with the conviction of the tanner.

slain in front of him. Graham himself was then hanged and his body cut into quarters. A fellow conspirator, the Earl of Atholl, was set in a pillory and repeatedly crowned with a red-hot crown inscribed 'The King of Traitors'. The following day he was bound and dragged through the streets. On the third and final day of his torment, he was fastened to a plank and disembowelled while still alive. His heart was torn out and thrown into a fire, and his head was cut off and stuck on the end of a pole.

SEEKING SANCTUARY

'I order and establish for ever,' vowed Edward the Confessor in Westminster Abbey, 'that what person, of what condition or estate soever he be, from whence soever he come, for what offence or cause it be, enter for his refuge into this holy place, he be assured of his life, liberty and limbs ...'

In all Christian countries a fugitive could seek sanctuary in a church. Safe from pursuit, the fugitive could elect to confess his crime to a coroner. A statute of 1284 laid down that, when this had been done, 'The Felon shall be brought out unto the Church Door, and a Sea Port shall be assigned him by the Coroner, and then he shall abjure the realm ...'

Sanctuary was sometimes violated. In 1378 Robert Hanley escaped from the Tower of London and was pursued as far as Westminster Abbey by the Constable of the Tower and several men-at-arms. Hanley rushed into the Abbey, but the Constable followed with drawn sword, and killed Hanley while Mass was being said. The pope was furious: the Constable and all those with him at the time of the murder were excommunicated, and Westminster Abbey was closed for four months.

OUTSIDE THE LAW Opponents of Edward II execute Hugh le Despenser, a royal favourite, in 1326.

ENTERTAINMENT IN THE MIDDLE AGES

When the time came to celebrate, there was plenty of choice – street theatres, sports, jousting, fairs, processions. There were minstrels, strolling players, dancing bears, jugglers, showmen with trained apes ... and if the harvest had been good, there were feasts and banquets.

Mystery plays, re-enacting the Biblical stories of the Creation, Noah's Flood, the Miracle at Cana and many others added a religious flavour to the festivities.

PAGEANTS AND PLAYS

From cockfights to mystery plays, from wandering minstrels to violent

games of football, people flocked to entertainments in city streets and on village greens –

despite the frequent and withering condemnation of the Church.

PEOPLE IN THE MIDDLE AGES played as hard as they worked. Hawking and hunting were the passions of kings and nobles: the most famous treatise on falconry was written by Emperor Frederick II in the 13th century and that on hunting by Gaston, Comte de Foix. Courtly literature abounds with references to the two sports. Deer were also hunted with crossbows, a sport in which ladies participated. Archery was popular and, as with most games and sports, provided an opportunity to gamble. Fishing and physical exercises, such as running, jumping and wrestling, were practised by all, though football – 'nothing but beastly fury and extreme violence,' as the 15th-century English diplomat Thomas Elyot called it – seems to have been a lower-class or schoolboy activity.

Many other entertainments were available in towns and in the larger villages: cockfighting and bear-baiting were popular, and performing animals and troupes of minstrels frequently toured the 'provinces'. But gentlemen's amusements were mainly made by members of their household: singing, playing the lute or harp, and acting in 'disguisings'. By the 15th century, backgammon, chess and dice were popular, although a newer amusement – playing cards – was beginning to replace them as a pastime for the long, badly lit winter evenings.

Medieval life was a series of battles – against disease, starvation, invasion and exploitation, but there was another battle: between the Church and the people over recreation. Actors were regarded as rogues, for they wore disguises, which enabled them to steal and commit other crimes with impunity. Indeed, there were two occasions when actors or mummers were suspected of plots to assassinate the English king – Edward II and Richard II. At the same time, medieval preachers condemned dancing, an evil pastime which allowed women to bewitch men and entice them from their prayers. Dancing, it was alleged, led to 'unclean kyssynge, clippynge and other unhonest handlynges'. Robert Manning of Brunne, in his treatise *Handlyng Synne* published in 1303, accused the common people of enjoying 'idle plays and japes, carolings, making of fool countenances …'

Plays and pageants acted in church buildings were a different matter, but by the 12th century, the Church was losing its control even over these performances,

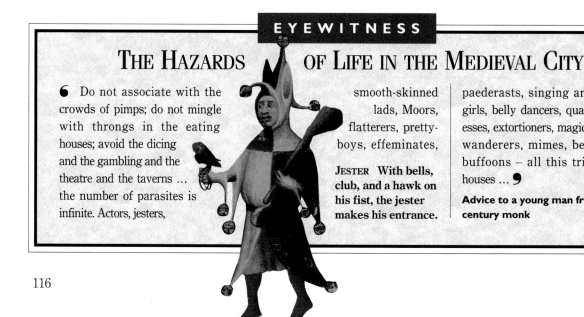

EYEWITNESS

THE HAZARDS OF LIFE IN THE MEDIEVAL CITY

❛ Do not associate with the crowds of pimps; do not mingle with throngs in the eating houses; avoid the dicing and the gambling and the theatre and the taverns … the number of parasites is infinite. Actors, jesters, smooth-skinned lads, Moors, flatterers, pretty-boys, effeminates, paederasts, singing and dancing girls, belly dancers, quacks, sorceresses, extortioners, magicians, night-wanderers, mimes, beggars and buffoons – all this tribe fill the houses … ❜

JESTER With bells, club, and a hawk on his fist, the jester makes his entrance.

Advice to a young man from a 12th-century monk

HOLY DRAMA A mystery play, the martyrdom of St Apollonia, is enacted in 15th-century France and a troupe of players and musicians with drum and bell (right) perform a dance.

much to the disgust of the Abbess of Hohenberg in Germany. 'What is presented in churches in our time?' she asked. 'Not a pattern of religious or divine veneration and a source of reverence, but the impassioned licence of irreligion and dissoluteness is produced ... The House of God is turned upside down by the mixing of laity and clergy, revelries, drunken orgies, buffooneries, harmful jests, plays in which weapons clash and only please the performers ...'

The Abbess was wrong in at least one of her criticisms. It was not only the performers who enjoyed the pageants. To the hard-working peasants and townsfolk they were occasions of wild delight. The towns of Europe were thronged with entertainers: jongleurs, mime troupes, gleemen (singers), troubadours, satirical *goliardi* (jesters), comedians, dancers, instrumentalists, tellers of tales, clowns, fools, sots, magicians and minstrels.

There was drama everywhere in the Middle Ages – in churches, inns, streets, or on the backs of wagons visiting villages. The greatest dramatic presentations of all, however, were the Mystery Plays, performed in all the major towns and cities to celebrate the feast of Corpus Christi early in June.

THE MYSTERY PLAYS

These works consisted of three groups: true Mystery Plays (religious plays based on Bible stories), miracle plays (based on the lives of the saints) and morality plays (original and allegorical stories based on conflicts between virtue and vice, truth and falsehood, and good and evil).

The Mystery Plays told the story of the Bible from the Creation or the Fall of Lucifer to the Day of Judgement. Each scene or 'pageant' was acted by a different group of actors to remind people of their places in the divine order of Creation. Favourite

DOOMED TO DAMNATION

❛ There are three types of *histriones* [actors]. Some transform and transfigure their bodies with lewd dancing and postures, either by stripping off their clothing, or by putting on dreadful masks, and all such are doomed to damnation, unless they leave their occupation. There are others besides who have no profession, but act in a reprehensible way, having no fixed abode; they follow after the courts of great ones and say scandalous and disgraceful things about those who are not there, in order to please the others. And indeed such men are damned, because the Apostle forbids us to eat food with such people, and such buffoons are called vagrants, since they are good for nothing except gobbling up food and amusing people. There is still a third type of *histriones*, those who have musical instruments to delight mankind, and frequent public drinking sessions and licentious gatherings, and there they sing diverse songs to urge men to wantonness ...❜

Thomas de Cabham, Sub-Dean of Salisbury Cathedral, 14th century

pageants depicted Adam and Eve, Noah and the Flood, Cain and Abel, the Annunciation, the Passion and the Resurrection. In towns, the Mystery Plays were strictly controlled, the staging of each pageant being entrusted to a different parish church or guild, all of whom met the cost of their own pageant and used it as an opportunity to advertise their skills and wares. In most cases there was a clear link between the guild and the pageant. The Guild of Water Drawers and Carriers staged *Noah and the Flood*; the Fishmongers, *Jonah and the Whale*; the Goldsmiths, *The Pageant of the Three Kings*; the Bakers, *The Last Supper*; the Vintners, *The Miracle at Cana*; the Drapers, *Paradise*, for Paradise was always a curtained area

hung with beautiful drapes. Less obvious, perhaps, was the contribution of the Guild of Plumbers, who staged *The Woman Taken in Adultery*.

The plays processed through the city, being repeated at a dozen or more sites. Since there were nearly 50 different pageants to be performed, the Mystery Plays took all day and employed a cast of hundreds. Large wagons were used as stages, each wagon having two levels: a lower screened level where the actors could rest and change their costumes, and a higher level on which they performed. The street itself

STREET THEATRE
Musicians with
bagpipes, bells,
drum and viol;
dancers; and actors
performing a play
with a holy theme –
all contribute to the
enjoyment of the
watching crowd.

A YEAR OF FESTIVALS

Each month of the medieval year was filled with festivals. Here is how they would have been celebrated in a typical hall or village.

January: Twelfth Night

The turn of the year was celebrated with dancing and a visit from the mummers to perform *The Visit of the Magi*. Revellers wore masks, disguising themselves as birds, oxen or deer. Large Twelfth Cakes (or *gateaux des rois*) were served, made of eggs and almonds and flavoured with honey. The drink was Lamb's Wool – cider, wine or beer heated with sugar, nutmeg and ginger. Roasted apples, floating on the surface, burst open to produce the white pulp that gave the drink its name.

JANUARY Revellers in a tavern.

February: St Valentine's Day

This was the Festival of Love – when the celebrants wore heart-shaped jewellery or embroidered hearts on their sleeves. Bowls of rosewater were sprinkled with crushed rosemary, basil and bay leaves to produce a gentle perfume. Pheasant, partridge and quail were served at table, and omelettes made of goose and sparrow's eggs, washed down with cups of Valentine wine. There was dancing, and a set

FEBRUARY A banquet in France.

of pairing games where the players sat in a circle, passing a ball from one to another behind their backs. One player sat in the middle and had to guess who held the ball. If he or she guessed correctly, then 'the pair' was made: if the guess was incorrect, he or she swapped places with the person wrongly chosen.

March: Easter

The Mystery Plays were performed in towns and cities, and even in country areas, itinerant players acted versions of the Bible stories. On Good Friday the plays were of a sombre nature, depicting Christ's Crucifixion and 'Crawling to the Cross', but on Easter Monday there was a joyous performance of the *Resurrection*. Dancing in the square or on the green celebrated the coming of spring.

April: All Fools' Day

This was the festival when the world turned upside down and the jester reigned. In France, students took over from their teachers, the young ruled the old, and the lowest

at table were served first. Many priests entered into the spirit of the festival by reciting the Holy Mass backwards, and people sent notes to each other in mirror writing.

May: May Day

This was the first truly outdoor festival of the year: dancing round the Maypole and crowning the Queen of the May with a golden crown and a single gold leaf; hanging wreaths of fresh green boughs on the doors of every house; eating Jack-in-the-Greens (large gingerbread biscuits decorated with sprigs of parsley); running races and rolling hoops.

June: Midsummer Eve

This was a festival of fire – Beltane Fire – when people lit huge outdoor pyres fuelled by animal bones (hence 'bone-' or 'bon-fire'). The mummers returned, to perform short plays of the deeds of St Michael, the Crusaders in the Holy Land, or St George. There was singing and

MAY Boating on a river.

dancing, and cuckoo-foot ale (wine spiced with ginger and basil).

July: St Swithin's Day

This was an anxious time for everyone, for it was said that if it rained on St Swithin's Day, it would be wet for the next 40 days.

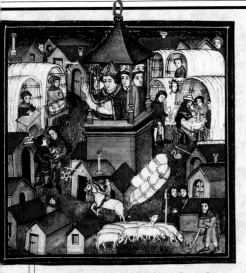

JUNE **Annual fair and market.**

August: Lammas Day
Even the animals shared in the celebrations on Lammas Day. The gates were opened for sheep and cattle to graze in fields and meadows that had been shut to them for most of the year. For the people, it was a welcome break in the harvest. In the morning one unfortunate sheep or ram was set completely free and the villagers had to catch it. If they were successful, the poor beast became the centre-piece of a grand evening feast.

September: Michaelmas
In honour of St Michael, the champion of the Christian faith, this was celebrated all over Europe. It was said that eating roast goose at Michaelmas would bring good luck. If no goose was available, people roasted chicken covered in goose feathers – or a 'goose' made of pastry and marzipan.

October: All Souls' Day
The end of October marked the end of summer and the end of the ancient year. Pagan festivals, such as the Day of the Dead, were replaced with Christian festivals,

such as All Souls' Day. Children went from door to door, singing and begging for soul cakes – flat, oval-shaped biscuits flavoured with currants, cinnamon and nutmeg. People lit bonfires in castle halls, where 'King Crispin' and the Revellers held court. The Revellers wore gowns of purple, with gold boots embroidered on them.

November: St Catherine's Day
St Catherine was the patron saint of lawyers, wheelwrights, ropemakers, carpenters, spinners and women students. Her feast day was

JULY **Sheep shearing.**

celebrated in the hall: jugglers threw flaming torches to and fro (Catherine wheels); a giant candle was placed in the centre of the room; and all took it in turns to leap over the candle without extin-

guishing the flame. There were wheel-shaped cakes rich with caraway seeds to eat, and cups of Lamb's Wool to drink. The day's festivities ended with a massive firework display.

SEPTEMBER **Treading grapes.**

December: Christmas
The festivities were opened by the Surveyor of Ceremonies, dressed all in green, who collected a coin from each of the assembled wassailers (revellers). The mummers returned to perform *The Play of the Three Shepherds*, after which the feasting began. The Yule log, the biggest piece of timber that could be found, was burnt in the hearth. In all but the poorest of medieval households there was *frumenty* to eat – a mixture of boiled milk, eggs, honey and spices. There was perry (a sweet pear wine) to drink, as well as posset made of milk, egg, ale and nutmeg.

DECEMBER **A snowball fight adds fun to the winter streets.**

A Day at the Michaelmas Fair

EVERY MICHAELMAS, a huge glove hung from the top of the Guildhall in many English towns. It was 10 feet long, and made of leather, with rags and wood chippings used as stuffing for the thumb and fingers. This was the sign that the Michaelmas Fair was about to begin, and all sellers and buyers were welcome. It was also a sign that the traders who attended the fair would be expected to contribute at least part of their profits to charity. Trains of packhorses came from all over the country as merchants brought their glassware, jewellery, suits of armour and fur cloaks. Local farmers brought their cheese and butter, poultry and vegetables. Horsetraders brought ponies and carthorses. Quacks brought tinctures and ointments.

The fair was set in a field or market square. It was noisy, with sellers shouting their wares, and musicians, players, jugglers and acrobats calling to the people to come and see them perform. There was much to guard against – thieves, cutpurses, pickpockets, forgers, rogues and some of the traders themselves. A special court was often set up for the day, called the Court of Pie Powder (from the French *pied poudre* – meaning 'dusty feet', for travellers to the fair would have dusty feet after trudging along the roads).

There was plenty to eat, with stalls that sold pies and sweetmeats, bowls of frumenty and posset, and mugs of ale and cider. There was much to wonder at, too: men who swallowed fire, lifted huge weights, escaped from ropes and chains, swallowed live rats, and bent the blades of swords. And, of course, there were fights and arguments – about the price of a goose, or the quality of a piece of cloth, or the weight of a bag of grain.

was often used to represent hell. Costumes were elaborate, and coloured to represent the virtues: white for purity, red for courage, and green for truth. People dressed up as devils wore black leather, horns, hoofs and tails, and carried wooden forks. God wore white leather, white hair and a long white beard. Death was particularly fearsome: 'a man dressed in close-fitting yellow leather so that his body and his head looked like those of a skeleton, all gaunt and fleshless without eyes, looking very ugly and very terrifying …'

The guild members went to great lengths to bring realism to the staging of the plays. Clouds of smoke, fireworks and the banging of pots and pans depicted hell; boughs, silks, fruits, fragrant flowers and blossoms created the Garden of Eden. Audiences delighted in the special effects: a three-headed serpent coiled round a tree, for example; dragons and gryphons that breathed fire; and artificial donkeys that dropped piles of manure as they were wheeled through the streets. Much ox-blood was used in scenes of execution, murder or battle. At a performance in Metz in 1437, a special harness was made so that Judas could hang himself while on stage, but the poor cleric playing the part was left hanging too long and almost died.

Professional actors were used in important roles, though most players were priests, guild members or townsfolk. It was hard work – actors playing the part of Jesus were sometimes tied to the Cross for three hours. Women were not often used, as it was felt that they lacked the vocal strength to project their lines, but one woman playing the part of St Catherine in a miracle play in Metz in 1468 had to learn over 2300 lines, and spoke 'with such feeling and so piteously that she provoked several people to tears'.

MERRYMAKING A 15th-century astronomical treatise illustrates that not all festivals were religious.

MIND, BODY AND SPIRIT

The Middle Ages were a period of curiosity, experiment and occasional discovery.

Scholars charted the earth and the heavens,

questioned the absolute authority of Church and king, raised great buildings,

produced beautiful books, exploited the fertility of the land –

but they still believed in magic and demons, in witchcraft and

a stone that would turn base metals into gold …

It did not matter what people did: the plague raged through Europe for two years, peaking in the summer of 1349. In fact, it was not one plague, but three: bubonic plague, brought by the rats and their fleas on the ships that had entered Messina; pneumonic plague, which was more infectious and could be contracted by inhalation; and septicaemic plague, which was more fatal than the other two, and was carried from victim to victim by fleas.

HEALTH AND DISEASE

The Black Death discredited much of the medical community. For hundreds of years, physicians had been trained in theory only, attending over 100 lectures on the teachings of Hippocrates alone during their university training. They believed in studying three aspects of the patient to produce a diagnosis: his urine, pulse rate and astrological profile. The key to the analysis of the liver was the colour, texture, odour and taste of the urine. A sample was taken from the patient and compared with dozens of other samples the physician kept in flasks. These were graded in colour from white to red, and corresponded to the 'four humours' – white phlegm, yellow bile, black bile and red blood. From this it was possible to tell whether the patient was of a sanguine, phlegmatic, choleric or melancholy temperament. Blood-letting then reduced the intensity of a particular humour.

TENDING WOUNDS Patients with an assortment of complaints attend a 15th-century French surgeon's clinic. A 13th-century manuscript (right) shows a neck wound being stitched.

MEDIEVAL CURES AND TREATMENTS

A cure for the plague

❦ I'll tell you what our bishop said to me the other day. Finding no relief from all the doctors, he says a poor person gave him a remedy which cured him immediately; namely, take a well-cooked onion, crush it with butter, and apply it to the tumour. Don't fool around with pills, because Maestro Bernardino [a prominent physician] ate a bushel of them and died anyway …❧

From a letter of Ser Lapo Mazzei, a Florentine notary, in 1400

A treatment for the blood flux

❦ For the blood flux, take a yarrow and wey bread and stamp them in a mortar, and take the juices of them and fair flow of wheat and temper them together and make a cake and bake it in ashes and make the sick eat it as hot as he may suffer it …❧

15th-century treatment for a stomach disorder

HERBAL REMEDIES A page in a 12th-century herbal reveals the virtues of henbane.

More time was spent, however, in compiling an astrological profile of the patient. The physician took the patient's name, age, sex and other statistics; gave them a numerical value; related this number to the appropriate astral conditions; and made his diagnosis by means of arithmetical calculations. Each part of the body was represented by a Zodiacal sign:

Aries – the head	*Cancer* – the lungs
Gemini – the chest	*Virgo* – the abdomen
Leo – the stomach	*Scorpio* – the genitalia
Libra – the lower abdomen	*Sagittarius* – the thighs
Aquarius – the calves	*Capricorn* – the knees
Taurus – the neck	*Pisces* – the ankles

It was not considered advisable to treat that part of the body during the month when its sign was in the ascendant: the lungs, for example, were not to be treated during July.

The failure of physicians to deal with the plague led to the increased use of surgery to combat disease and, from the 13th century onwards, surgeons accompanied troops marching to battle, so there were no shortage of patients on whom they could experiment, or of corpses on the battlefield that they could dissect without interference from civil or ecclesiastical authorities. Surgeons (educated through apprenticeship rather than at university) were called on more and more to remove stones, lymph glands (in case of scrofula), fistulas and ulcers; to dress wounds with white of egg and finely ground flour; to straighten, stretch and set broken bones; and to treat cancer and hernias. Treatment was brutal and without anaesthetic. Patients were in agony during most operations, and of those who survived the knife, 50 per cent died of post-operative infection.

Surgeons had several other methods of treating their patients. Like physicians, they used bleeding. The favoured parts of the body were the arms, neck, nose, chest, back, hips, knees and feet. Leeches were commonly used, as these were less dangerous; they were carefully selected, with green or lime-coloured leeches from frog ponds preferred to black ones. These were starved for a day before being applied to the wound or a spot on the body that had been rubbed until raw. Drugs were also used by surgeons, in the form of pills, potions, powders, balms, salves and ointments; those to be taken internally were often mixed with sweetmeats or wine. Purgatives and enemas were also often used. It was recommended that at least two dozen types of wound

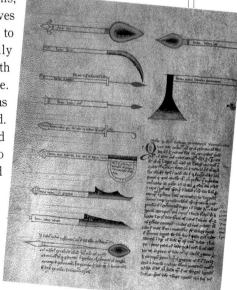

MEDICAL HANDBOOK A page from an early treatise on medicine shows a variety of surgical instruments.

or ailment were treated by 'cautery' – the application of a hot iron to the part of the body infected. This treatment was thought best for infections of the neck, chest, stomach, wrists, knees, ankles and shoulder-blades. Both physicians and surgeons used cupping – the placing of heated cups over shallow incisions made in the patient's body. As in bleeding, cupping was thought to draw out infection and bad blood.

BAD HUMOURS Blood-letting was a popular cure-all.

In the late 15th century new studies of anatomy and physiology allowed physicians to regain some of the ground they had lost to surgeons. At the same time, many new medical textbooks were published. The finest medical schools were in Italy, a country where demonstration had replaced lectures, where doctors already specialised, and where surgeons and physicians worked together. There were fewer than 1000 patients per doctor in Florence. By the 15th century, at least some of these new ideas and practices had begun to spread throughout Europe.

THE MEDICAL TRADE

For many years after the Black Death a variety of tradesmen were allowed to practise surgery, including fullers, tailors, weavers and wax-makers. Barbers, however, had been acting as surgeons for hundreds of years. They advertised their medical role by tying bloody rags to poles outside their shops, or by placing buckets of blood in the window (to show that they 'let' blood). A great many of these unlicensed medical practitioners were charlatans.

Apothecaries were regarded as little more than high-class grocers. Many of them were of Italian origin, for Italy was the centre of the European spice trade, and apothecaries used spices in the manufacture of the drugs they sold to physicians and surgeons. Apothecaries were usually to be found only in towns and cities, while it was the unqualified physicians or 'leeches' who practised their trade in villages and rural areas.

Leeches were self-taught or trained by their parents or grandparents in the art of folk medicine. Like apothecaries, they compounded their own drugs and pastes, from animal, herbal and mineral bases, mixed with spices; some 'leech books' of the time included such monstrosities as a roasted fat cat stuffed with herbs and bear and hedgehog fat, which was recommended for the quinsy (inflammation of the tonsils). Nevertheless, leeches were competent enough in treating minor traumas and low-grade fevers and, because they were local people, they communicated well with their patients.

The only opportunity a woman had for practising medicine was as a village leech. Although women acted as midwives and supervised all childbirths, this tarnished their reputation as healers, for so many babies were stillborn and so many women died in childbirth. In Paris in 1322, five women were put on trial for practising as physicians. Although witnesses gave evidence that the women had successfully treated them where male doctors had failed, the Court

EYEWITNESS

TREATMENT FOR A ROYAL CONDITION

When King Henry VI of England suffered a mental breakdown in 1454, six doctors produced the following recommended treatment.

❛ Electuaries [powders mixed with honey or syrup], potions, syrups, confections, laxative medicines, clysters [enemas], gargles, baths, removal of the skin, fomentations [the application of hot flannels to the body], embrocations, shaving of the head, ointments, plasters, waxes, scarification [the cutting of small incisions in the body], with or without rubifacients [the application of heat], and whatever else is necessary ...❜

The king not only survived, but lived another 17 years before being put to death in the Tower of London.

APOTHECARIES Herbs and materials are gathered, weighed, ground and processed (left). They would have been sold in an apothecary's shop (above).

of Justice scorned such testimony, saying 'it is certain that a man approved in the aforesaid art could cure the sick better than any woman'. The five women were excommunicated for their crime.

THE COMING OF THE HOSPITAL

Nuns and monks housed and tended the sick throughout the Middle Ages, but the first secular hospitals were built in Florence in the 14th century, after the city had lost half its population in the Black Death. The hospitals were supported by funds from the commune, the guilds, religious orders, chivalric orders and private bequests. Women had full responsibility for the day-to-day administration of the wards. There were 100 beds in each ward, and every

bed had a mattress, bolster, pillows, linen and cover. On admission to the hospital, patients were examined by the woman in charge, their clothes were removed and stored under their names in cupboards. They were then issued with standard clothing and registered in the book of admissions. In a typical Florentine hospital, several doctors provided the medical care, and there was a resident apothecary to make up the drugs and potions prescribed. The drugs prescribed were entered in a drugs book under the bed number of the patient. Wards were general, but nobles, the wounded, priests and clerics, those mentally ill from 'physical causes', and victims of diseases involving skin lesions were isolated from the general ward and from each other.

Cristoforo Landino gave this description of the Hospital of Santa Maria Nuova in Florence in 1480: 'In it they care continuously for more than 300 invalids. Difficult as it is to arrange, the beds are always clean, and there is always someone to look after the patient and see to his needs. Food and medicine are not distributed indiscriminately, but to each individual according to his disease. Both physicians and surgeons are always on hand and give individual directions for all. As a result, many noble and rich foreigners, afflicted with some illness during a voyage, have chosen to be treated in this institution.'

THE MEDIEVAL MENAGERIE

Fables about an assortment of creatures, real and mythical, were used to instruct the people in Christian beliefs and values.

DEATH OF A LEGEND The mythical unicorn had to be lured to its death by a young virgin.

THE BESTIARY, or *Book of Beasts*, was second only to the Bible in popularity during the Middle Ages. Deriving from a Greek text called *Physiologus*, written in the 2nd century AD by an anonymous Christian ascetic living in Alexandria, it was a book of stories based on supposed 'facts' of natural science. In the 7th century it was enlarged by Isidore, Bishop of Seville, who added the wolf, ibex, dog, crocodile, owl and dragon to the 74 other creatures of the original manuscript. By the end of the 13th century, the Bestiary had been translated into Latin, Ethiopian, Syriac, Arabic, Coptic, Armenian, Anglo-Saxon, Italian, Slavic, Flemish, German and Icelandic.

Although most bestiaries were sumptuously illustrated, their main purpose was to reinforce spiritual and moral teaching through allegory. Texts stressed the importance of chastity, abstinence and obedience, with parallels drawn between the world of nature and episodes in the life of Christ. So, for example, three 'natures' were attributed to the lion, 'king of the beasts': if a lion scented a hunter, it swept away its own tracks with its tail; when it was asleep, its eyes stayed open; and 'when the lioness bears her cubs, she gives birth to them dead, and watches over them until after three days their father breathes in their faces and brings them back to life'. These three 'natures' reminded the reader that Christ covered his tracks against the Devil; that, though He died on the Cross, He remained ever vigilant; and that, after three days, He was raised from the dead by God the Father.

Some of the allegories were more picturesque. The panther was said to have spicy breath which attracted all animals except for the dragon, just as Christ's 'sweetness' draws all mankind to Him. Many of the animal characteristics in later fables were first attributed to them in the Bestiary. The fox was cunning; the crocodile, hypocritical; the ant, industrious; and the hyena, untrustworthy and evil, for it imitated human voices to lure honest people from their homes at night.

The Bestiary included a number of mythical creatures. Among them was the unicorn, which could only be trapped if 'a virgin girl is sent off alone into the woods; as soon as it sees her, it leaps into her lap and embraces her – so it is caught by the hunters'. The griffin, which was thought to come from the deserts of India, was half-lion and half-eagle; the man-eating manticore

TRANSLATED INTO STONE A carved column decorated with mythical creatures such as the dragon, griffin, unicorn and manticore.

BEATING THE DEVIL The ship of righteousness races against a sea monster. **Right:** The lion breathes life into his cubs.

had a lion's body, a scorpion's tail, the head of a man and a triple row of teeth.

But perhaps the most important of them all was the phoenix, whose existence was held to be a proof that Christ rose from the dead. There was only one

phoenix – or so the story went – and it lived in India. When 500 years old, the bird flew to Heliopolis in Egypt. Here, a funeral pyre was prepared which the phoenix itself ignited by sparking its beak on a stone; the bird then fanned the flames with its wings and was quickly reduced to ashes. The next day a small worm-like creature was to

ILLUMINATING TALES
Great care was taken over the illustrations in medieval bestiaries, such as this mid-13th century example.

be seen in the ashes; this assumed the shape of a bird with feathers on the following day, and on the third day it flew all the way back to India.

Apart from their use as the text for many sermons, bestiaries also had an influence on medieval art. The illustrations in bestiaries were copied into other manuscripts, and griffins, basilisks, dragons and serpents found their way into frescoes, paintings and carvings in churches and public buildings throughout Europe.

THE OBSESSION WITH DEATH

In an age when life was cheap and death was always close,

some people sought salvation by doing good works. But for many, the pain and suffering on

earth were no more than a prelude to the hell fires of eternal damnation.

ISEASE, starvation, war and plague meant that death was an ever-present concern of people in the Middle Ages. Many were not so much afraid of death itself as of the eternal damnation that would come to all who died in sin. Hell, with its furnaces and its souls writhing in torment, was a very real place – to be seen in lurid paintings and carvings in many churches and cathedrals. More important than the quality of life on earth was preparation for the life to come. Salvation had to be earned – by good deeds, by purity, by atonement and by penitence. Rich and poor alike, powerful and humble, temporal and spiritual – all had to earn their heavenly rewards.

On December 29, 1170, four knights of the king's household – Reginald Fitz Urse, William de Tracy, Hugh de Morville and Richard le Breton – believing that they were fulfilling the king's wishes, entered Canterbury Cathedral and murdered Thomas Becket, Archbishop of Canterbury. The crime was particularly horrendous by medieval standards. The Archbishop was a man of God, and the crime took place at the very altar of the cathedral. Henry II believed that only by undergoing an ordeal prescribed by the Church could he obtain God's forgiveness.

Prior to the penance, Henry fasted for several days.

On the appointed morning, he put on a hair shirt and pilgrim's robes. He then walked barefoot from the church of St Dunstan in Canterbury to the cathedral, leaving behind a trail of bloody footsteps. At the cathedral he made a full confession before kneeling at the martyr's shrine to receive five strokes with birchrods from the priests and three strokes from each of the 80 monks. Following this, he prayed all night, prostrate on the stone floor of the cathedral.

Henry then returned to London, where he fell ill with a fever. As he recovered, he learnt that the Scots had been defeated and that a fleet set to invade England had been driven back by storms. It seemed that God had relented.

THE FLAGELLANTS

There were many occasions throughout the Middle Ages, however, when there was little evidence of such divine grace. Many saw the Black Death as a punishment from God on a sinful world. The Brotherhood of Flagellants, for example, believed self-flagellation was the only way to obtain God's forgiveness. They went from town to town, in groups of hundreds at a time, stripped to the waist and whipping themselves with scourges. The rules of the brotherhood were strict. They were forbidden to

---

EYEWITNESS

1376: A SLEEPING POWDER 'USED BY ROGUES'

❝ A powder to make a man sleep against his will, used by rogues and vagabonds who fell into company along the road with pilgrims so that they may rob them of their silver when they are asleep: "Take equal quantities of seed of henbane, darnel, black poppy, and dried bryony root; pound it together in a brass mortar very fine. Put some in his soup, or in a piece of bread, or in his drink, and he shall sleep at once, whether he wishes to or not, all day or longer according to the amount that has been given to him …❞

**From the *Treatises* of Fistula,
14th century**

wash, shave, sleep in beds, talk, change their clothes or have sexual intercourse without the consent of their master. As they grew in numbers, the flagellants made greater claims for the importance of their gruesome crusade. They were acting for everyone, they said, expiating the sins of the world.

The flagellants also used their power and influence to persecute the Jewish communities all over Europe. It was rumoured that the plague had been started by the Jews, and that they had deliberately poisoned wells to destroy good Christians. In France, Spain, Italy and Germany, Jews were massacred in their thousands: 12,000 in Mainz alone. At last the Pope acted. A Papal Bull of October 1349 ordered the dispersal of the flagellants. The Holy Roman Emperor forbade public flagellation on pain of death. They were arrested and put to death. Almost as suddenly as they had emerged, the flagellants disappeared, 'like night phantoms or mocking ghosts', according to Henry of Hereford, a contemporary chronicler.

As the plague returned year after year in the 14th and 15th centuries, people became obsessed by the concept of death. A new form of street theatre developed – the *Danse Macabre,* or Dance of Death. The dancers portrayed society as divided into 14 pairs, a mixture of clergy and laity. The Pope was paired with the Holy Roman Emperor, cardinal with king, patriarch with constable, and so on down to priest with peasant,

DEATHBED SCENES A dying man (above) is attended by family and retainers while his heir, at the bottom, checks his inheritance. The forces of good and evil (left) fight for the soul of a dying man.

friar with child, and clerk with hermit. A 15th-century poet, Jean le Fevre, wrote verses to accompany the dance: 'Advance, see yourselves in us, dead, naked, rotten and stinking. So will you be ... Power, honour, riches are naught; at the hour of death only good works count ...'

The dance was portrayed in sculpture and painting. Sermons concentrated on death, and religious art lost its serenity. Death became a murderous figure – the 'grim reaper' – wielding a scythe. Carvings on tombs concentrated on the putrefaction of the flesh, on worms, maggots and decay. Death's head masks and body moulds were taken from the corpses of the famous and the devout.

Everyone was aware of the 'purifying pains of

PILGRIMAGE: THE GREAT ADVENTURE OF THE MIDDLE AGES

THE DEVOUT, the desperate and the delinquent were all found among the bands of pilgrims who took up the scrip (a wallet for food) and the burdon (a pilgrim staff, roughly 5 feet long).

The greatest pilgrimage of all was to the Holy Land. In the 15th century, an English pilgrim, William Wey, a Fellow of Eton College, took ship from Venice where he bought a bed, mattress, two pillows, two pairs of sheets and a quilt from a dealer in St Mark's Square. He then bought wine, fresh water and biscuits, and a chest in which he stored bread, cheese, fruit, eggs, bacon, laxatives, ginger, rice, figs, raisins, pepper, saffron, cloves, mace, a frying pan, dishes, platters, wooden saucers, cups and a bread grater.

But there were many other destinations, and the pilgrims would buy souvenir badges of lead or cloth from each shrine they visited: shells from Santiago de Compostella, for example, or miniature heads of St John the Baptist from Amiens, or St Veronica's napkin from Rome.

The pilgrims travelled by established routes, resting at hostels, monasteries and hospices. Some of these offered little more than boards to sleep on, but others had baths, comfortable rooms and good food. As early as the 12th century, guide books were published giving details of the lodgings available on the way. One of the first was the *Guide to Pylgrimes to St Jacques* (Santiago de Compostella). Some pilgrims trav-

OUTRAGE The murder of Thomas Becket (above) made Canterbury a shrine. The deed is also depicted on this French reliquary (left).

elled alone, others in the company of strangers, but a few travelled in style. When Nicolò d'Este journeyed to the Holy Land in 1417, he took with him a doctor, four waiters, a chaplain, a purser, a cook and under-cook, a tailor, a barber, two trumpeters, a page and a scribe.

The pilgrims stopped to pray at shrines on the way, carving their initials and names on the walls of chapels and churches, and occasionally vandalising sacred works of art. There was intense competition among cities as to which held the most relics. Venice boasted an extraordinary array, which included the arm of St George; the roasted flesh of St Lawrence 'albeit turned to powder'; the ear of St Paul; one of the jars of wine miraculously transformed from water by Christ in the wedding at Cana; and one of Goliath's teeth ('know you, more than half a foot long, and weighs twelve pounds'). At other shrines, pilgrims worshipped Christ's milk tooth, his umbilical cord and even his blood.

PILGRIMS A 15th-century lady (above) offers refreshments to returning pilgrims. Some of them probably carry metal souvenirs of their journeys (left).

purgatory' and was taught that 'three things helpen souls most out of penance, that is devout praying, alms-giving and mass singing.' Even the poorest would hope for the prayers of their families or the communal prayers of their parish on All Souls' Day; the rather better-off souls could hope for those of their fellow members of religious guilds as well; while the rich could leave money for prayers and Masses to be said by a priest specifically paid for the purpose. The very rich might try to found a chantry, hospital or college which would be endowed primarily to provide prayers in perpetuity for the founder.

BUYING A TICKET TO HEAVEN

Another way of ensuring salvation was to buy or earn a pardon or an indulgence. A pardon could be bought from a pardoner, one empowered by the Pope to travel from town to town selling absolution from sin, remittance from penance and freedom from fasting or vows of chastity. Much of the money raised was pocketed by the pardoners themselves, but the Church approved the system as at least some of the takings financed its other work.

The purchase of an indulgence did not bring absolution from any past sin, but bought future relief from the years of purgatory that awaited any soul before entering into heaven. The papacy, it was claimed, had an inexhaustible treasury of merit, on which sinners could draw by acquiring indulgences. The value of an indulgence lay in the number of years' relief from purgatory that it represented. For example, one sight of the napkin with which St Veronica had wiped Christ's face on his way to the Crucifixion, earned a pilgrim to Rome 12,000 years' indulgence. For a citizen of Rome, the same sight earned only 3000 years' indulgence.

Pardons and indulgences were increasingly bought rather than earned, and the abuse of the system was criticised more and more – as in Chaucer's *The Pardoner's Tale*. What had originally been conceived by the Church as a way to salvation had, by the end of the Middle Ages, become one of the main causes of the Protestant Reformation in the 16th century.

INTERMENT **A corpse is wrapped in a winding sheet (above) before being placed in the coffin. A priest (right) presides at the graveside ceremony.**

A Benedictine Monastery

Benedictine Monasteries, such as this 13th-century one, flourished throughout northern and western Europe from the 9th to the 15th centuries. The monasteries were in many cases large communities, almost as big as a medieval town and equally self-sufficient. There was a bakehouse, a brewery, an orchard and gardens where the monks cultivated peas, beans, leeks and parsnips, in addition to a range of medicinal herbs.

As well as the prior, sub-prior and deans of order, who controlled the running of the monastery and the discipline of the monks, each monastery had a variety of specialists: a precentor (in charge of music), a chancellor (in charge of the library), a bursar (in charge of the supplies and accounts), a cellarer (in charge of meat and victuals), a terrar or hostillar (who acted as land agent and supervisor of the monastery's guest house), a chamberlain (in charge of clothes), a refectorian (in charge of the dining hall), a commoner (who supplied the monks with the tools of their work – from pens and ink to spades and hayforks), a master of the infirmary (who looked after old and sick monks) and an almoner (who was in charge of the distribution of alms from the monastery to the local poor). Throughout the Middle Ages, monks kept alive the tradition of illuminated manuscripts.

Since many monasteries were built in remote locations, pilgrims, travellers, and even fugitives saw them as places of refuge or as stopping points where they could expect food and lodging for a night's rest from their journey. The merchants had their own luxurious quarters.

Orchard

Abbey

Chapter house

Scriptorium

Infirmary

Latrines

Storehouse

Wash room

Refectory

Kitchen

Bakehouse

Vegetable garden

ewery

137

SCIENCE AND SUPERSTITION

It is hard to draw the borderline between what we now see as superstition –

alchemy and astrology, for example – and what was then viewed as science:

chemistry and astronomy.

THE MIDDLE AGES were a battleground between reason and authority, progressive thought and reactionary dogma. One of the greatest scholars of the 12th century, Peter Abelard, challenged the Church and its slavish devotion to the old ways of thinking. A brilliant poet and teacher, he rediscovered Aristotelian dialectic and made central to university teaching the art of disputation. He also read the works of the Arab scholars. 'I learned from my Arabian masters under the leading of reason,' he wrote. 'You, however, captivated by the appearance of authority, follow your halter. For what else should authority be called but a halter? Just as brute beasts are led where one wills by a halter, so authority of past writers leads not a few of you into danger.'

Most churchmen, however, regarded the likes of Abelard as purveyors of 'drool and dribble, unseasoned with the salt of philosophers'. It was dangerous to challenge the Church, and excommunication awaited many who raised their voices to proclaim that reason showed the teachings of the Church to be false. Many of the so-called new ideas were in actual fact revived from the works of

FOOL'S GOLD
To turn base metal into gold was the frustrated obsession of the alchemist.

the ancient Greek philosophers Plato and Aristotle, or of great Arab philosophers such as Averroes, who had brought methods of observation and dissection to the study of medicine and mankind. Other ideas were shockingly original, such as those of William of Ockham in the early 14th century, who claimed that the truths of religion could never be proved, or those of the religious reformers John Wycliffe in England and Jan Huss in Bohemia.

ALCHEMY AND ASTROLOGY

In addition to the wranglings of the theologians and some genuine breakthroughs in scientific thought, the field of ideas was dominated, throughout the Middle Ages, by 'sciences' such as alchemy (from which the word 'chemistry' derives) and astrology. Alchemy as

STATUS QUO A priest officiates at Mass in a manuscript attacking the reformer Wycliffe. A 15th-century edition of an Aristotelian work shows discontented craftsmen.

a study was introduced into western Europe by the Arabs. It was based on the four elements defined by Aristotle: earth, air, fire and water. Just as cold, wet water could be turned into hot, wet air, so, the alchemists believed, human bodies could be turned back into their original constituent elements, if only the catalyst or agent could be found to do this. This missing agent became known as the 'philosopher's stone'. Alchemy was obsessed with the search for this substance, for it was also believed that the philosopher's stone would turn base metal into gold or silver, and that it could be used to create an elixir of life that would bring immortality.

Alchemists were regarded with a mixture of awe, fear and loathing, as magicians in league with the devil. People were reluctant to visit an alchemist's laboratory – indeed, alchemists themselves discouraged visitors. Hunched over his jars and furnace (or *athanor*), the alchemist heated spherical containers, crucibles, flasks and retorts. The chemicals he used (sulphur and mercury) were no ordinary chemicals, and the symbols of the alchemist's trade were powerful and frightening: a 'king and queen' representing the sun and the moon; a grey wolf representing antimony (a metal with allegedly purifying properties); a wooden-legged man representing dull metal; and a fan of peacock's feathers representing the four humours of the body.

Two of the most famous medieval alchemists were Nicolas and Perrenelle Flammel, who announced early in the 14th century that they had uncovered an ancient book, 'a gilded book very old and very large, with a cover of brass, well bound, all engraven with letters of strange figures'. This book, they claimed, would finally lead to the discovery of the philosopher's stone. It did not.

There was also a nobler side to the work of the alchemists. Just as the philosopher's stone would turn base metals into gold, so they believed it would change the base instincts of men into nobler qualities. And, though many cheated their patrons, there were those alchemists who were genuinely convinced that their efforts would be of great benefit to mankind. In the words of Thomas Norton, a 15th-century alchemist:

The true men search and seek all alone
In hope to find the delectable stone,
And for that they would that no man should have loss,
They prove and seek all at their own cost.
So their own purses they will not spare
They make their coffers thereby full bare …

Astrology, too, was believed by many to influence the destiny and behaviour of mortals. Medieval astrologers taught that there were two types of heavenly body – the fixed star and the moving planet. Fixed stars controlled the immutable and unalterable laws of nature (the passing of the seasons, or the rhythm of day and night), and the planets controlled day-to-day events, such as the course of history, or birth and death.

Well-to-do families called in astrologers to compile

horoscopes for new-born children, for it was thought that the planets and stars would dictate the child's personality, life span and intelligence, and foretell whether he or she would grow up to be rich or poor, famous or obscure, happy or unhappy. The planets influenced the calling a child should follow in life. A boy born under Mars should become a smith or a soldier, and a boy born under Venus should aim for a career as an artist or courtier. Girls, on the other hand, were left with the choice of marriage or a nunnery.

New Theories of the Universe

The teachings of the Church, and the sciences of alchemy and astrology, came increasingly under attack during the Middle Ages. Nicole Oresme, Bishop of Lisieux in the 14th century, was a mathematician, astronomer and economist who distinguished astrology from astronomy, the true study of the stars and the heavens.

He created a machine that displayed the movements of the planets in the heavens, and gave an early and reasonably accurate explanation of the structure of the universe: 'The earth is round like a ball and philosophers say that the sphere of the world is made up of the heavens and the four elements. First comes the earth, massive and round, although not perfectly round, for there are mountains and valleys. But if the earth were viewed from the moon, it would appear to be round, and the eclipse of the moon, the result of the earth's shadow, shows the earth to be round. The earth is at the centre of the universe because it is the heaviest of the four elements ...'

Oresme and many others were, of course, wrong in assuming that the earth was the centre of the universe. Such a belief was a fundamental 'scientific' axiom of the ancient astronomer Ptolemy, accepted by pagans and Christians alike. It took another 200 years, and the publication of Nicolas Copernicus's *On the Revolution of the Celestial Orbs*, before people accepted that the planets revolve around the sun.

Medieval scientists were mistaken in many of their views. Oresme and others believed that the earth was surrounded by a watery sphere, above which were layers of air and fire – the four elements being in concentric harmony. Other astronomers wrote of spheres beyond these, so far away that their composition would never be discovered. But slowly and steadily, medieval scientists edged towards a greater understanding of the nature of the universe.

Their terrestrial horizons broadened, too. Despite Marco Polo's travels, the East was only dimly understood, but the west coast of Africa and the islands of the Azores, Madeira and the Canaries were all explored during the 1420s and 1430s.

Sorcery and Witchcraft

These advances did little to dispel traditional beliefs in sorcery and witchcraft, or in spells and superstitions (mice are the souls of murdered people, for example). Here is an example of an early medieval incantation to reduce an enemy to nothing:

May you be consumed as coal upon the hearth,
May you shrink as dung upon a wall, and may you
dry up as water in a pail.
May you become as small as a linseed grain,
and much smaller than the hipbone of an itch mite,
and may you become so small that you
become nothing.

For hundreds of years people had believed in secret gatherings of men and women who had sold their souls to the devil, and who practised the black arts. The witches met underground, they said, some bringing with them the bodies of children they had murdered.

Novices renounced the Christian faith by stamping on a crucifix, and then worshipped the master of the cult by kissing him on the buttocks. There followed feasting and drinking – or so the rumours continued – and a parody of the Eucharist, in which the bodies of the dead children were boiled with 'loathsome substances' to make an ointment. The witches coated their own bodies with this ointment, which gave them the power to fly.

What did change in medieval times, however, was the attitude of the Church and society towards witches. In the Dark Ages witches had been seen as unfortunate people, whose bodies and souls had been seized by the devil against their will. By the 11th century, however, witches were generally believed to have entered voluntarily into pacts with Lucifer, Satan or Beelzebub. And the crime was no longer mere sorcery or magic, but heresy. Witchcraft itself was punished as a heresy by burning, after trial in the church courts, though if the accusation included murder, the civil courts would be involved.

ADVICE FROM THE ASTROLOGERS

SIGNS OF THE ZODIAC Aries, Virgo, Libra and Sagittarius are illustrated in 15th-century manuscripts.

It was said that by studying the relative positions of the planets and the stars, the future could be foretold:

❛ If the Kalends of January shall be on the Lord's Day, the winter will be good and mild and warm; the spring windy, and the summer dry. Good vintage, increasing flocks, and honey will be abundant; the old men will die and peace will be made ...'

Similarly, the phases of the moon were said to have a great influence over people's lives. After a full moon:

On the first day: if any fall ill on this day, they will be sick for a long time. A child born on this day will be happy and prosperous.

On the second day: a good day to buy and sell, and a good day to begin a sea voyage ...

On the third day: a criminal is most likely to be caught if he commits a crime on this day.

On the fourth day: a good day to start building.

On the fifth day: a good day for women to conceive.

On the sixth day: the best day for hunting and fishing.

On the seventh day: a good day to meet and fall in love.

On the eighth day: if any fall sick on this day he shall most certainly die.

On the ninth day: do not let the moon shine on you this day or you ... shall go mad.

On the tenth day: any born on this day are destined to be wanderers and restless of spirit. ❜

Anonymous 14th-century manuscript

Between the 12th and 15th centuries, thousands of men and women, almost all of them innocent of anything more serious than challenging the views of the Church, were arrested, tortured (to make them name their evil associates), and then executed for heresy or witchcraft. A few were lucky enough to be tried by 'swimming'.

In this grotesque process, the arms and legs of an accused witch were fastened with rope and she was thrown into deep water. If the water of God rejected her and she floated, she was guilty of witchcraft. If she sank, God had received her and she was innocent. Luckier still were those tried by 'weighing'. Here, a suspected witch was placed on one side of a pair of scales, and a Bible on the other. If the witch was lighter than the Bible, then she was guilty.

Modern inventions such as printing did nothing to help witches. New ideas and theories were no more tolerant than the old. One of the earliest and most popular printed books was the *Malleus Maleficarum* ('The Hammer of Witches') of Jakob Sprenger and Heinrich Krämer, which was first published in Germany in 1484 with papal approval. It was claimed: 'What else is woman but a foe to friendship, an inescapable punishment, a necessary evil, a natural temptation, a desirable calamity, a domestic danger, a delectable detriment, an evil of nature ... The word woman is used to mean the lust of the flesh ... I have found a woman more bitter than death, and a good woman more subject to carnal lust ... She is an imperfect animal, she always deceives ... Women also have weak memories, and it is a natural vice in them not to be disciplined, but to follow their own impulses without any sense of what is due ... She is a liar by nature ... Let us also consider her gait, posture and habit, in which is vanity of vanities ...'

HOLY SHRINES AND RELICS

All over Europe, sick and healthy alike flocked on pilgrimages

to visit popular holy shrines and relics.

MAKING CONTACT with holy places and holy relics gained the poor sinner protection from danger, disease and the works of the Devil . . . or so the people of the Middle Ages believed. Every important church and shrine had the mortal remains of a saint or an object closely associated with a holy person. Rome had the remains of countless martyrs; in England, Canterbury had St Thomas Becket and Westminster the saint-king Edward the Confessor. Turin claimed to have the shroud of Christ (though there were already those who doubted its authenticity), and Ostia one of the stones that killed St Stephen. Aachen boasted the swaddling clothes and loin cloth of Christ and the raiment of John the

Baptist. The Spanish cathedral of Oviedo cherished a napkin, supposedly used as a pillow for Christ's head. Most of these relics – many of which were undoubtedly authentic, even if others were not – were regularly on show. Visitors were allowed to touch them, and many cottages held some small scrap of cloth that had been used to stroke a holy relic.

Until the 13th century, the Church officially endorsed the powers claimed for relics. Less approved by the Church, though equally popular, was the practice of carrying an amulet: a ring or brooch, a tiny gem-studded locket or case, or a small flask called an ampulla, containing something that reminded the bearer of Christ's teaching and love – a few

TURIN SHROUD Said to bear the image of Christ's face, this cloth drew crowds of pilgrims to Turin's Cathedral of St John the Baptist.

mustard seeds, perhaps (recalling Christ's parable in which he compared faith to a mustard seed), or a drop or two of holy oil. Such lucky charms were regarded as protecting the bearer against sickness or bad fortune: an amulet containing a fossilised spider, for instance, was thought to be good against fever; one containing wolf dung was said to be best against colic.

Talismans were prepared under the special influences of the sun, moon and planets. The zodiacal sign under which the talisman was fashioned, usually from wood or metal, determined whether its powers were beneficial or not, for talismans could be used for evil purposes, too. Soldiers wore talismans in the shape of a right hand when going into battle, since the hand was the symbol of God. Merchants wore ones in the shape of an open hand, which was believed to bring success in business deals. Many houses had a horseshoe nailed to an outside wall, the ends of the shoe pointing upwards – thought to be a talisman against evil and madness, or 'moon mania'.

HOLY RELICS A reliquary cross that belonged to Pope Urban V is said to contain a piece of Christ's bloodied robe. Above: An early 14th-century Italian reliquary diptych.

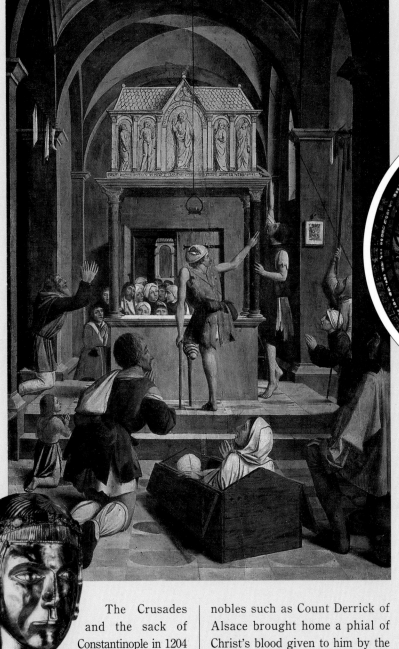

HEALING POWERS In this 15th-century painting, a group of pilgrims, many of them sick or injured, pray at the tomb of a saint in the hope of a miraculous cure for themselves or their loved ones.

JOURNEY'S END A pilgrim kneels and makes his offering at the tomb of Thomas Becket in Canterbury Cathedral.

GOLDEN SAINT An early 13th-century image of St Eustace is cast in gold and richly decorated. It comes from Germany.

The Crusades and the sack of Constantinople in 1204 increased the numbers of relics that were available. Rulers and nobles such as Count Derrick of Alsace brought home a phial of Christ's blood given to him by the Patriarch of Jerusalem. In 1239, Louis IX of France brought Christ's Crown of Thorns to the Cathedral of Notre Dame in Paris. In 1215 the Church banned the sale of relics, but to raise money it started selling indulgences, or pardons for sins committed. These were originally granted only to those who had gone on Crusade, but later they were also sold to those who made a pilgrimage to Rome. By the late 13th century, anyone with the money could buy an indulgence from a 'pardoner': along with an indulgence, one pardoner even sold a phial said to contain the sound of King Solomon's bells.

In the late Middle Ages, the Renaissance and later the Reformation, many preachers began to condemn relics. The reformers, in particular, were scathing in their attacks on even the holiest of them. If all the alleged remnants of the True Cross were put together, claimed John Calvin, they would make a 'good ship': the time for venerating 'filthy ragges, stinking bootes, gobbettes of wodde and such pelfrie' was over.

AN AGE OF LEARNING

Schools were few and far between; books were beautiful but scarce;

Latin was still the language of study. Then, in the 15th century, came the printing press –

a new way of disseminating new ideas.

 HE OPPORTUNITIES for education increased steadily during the Middle Ages, and by the 15th century, a substantial proportion of the population could read and most of the gentry and richer townsmen could write. Among the nobility a child was expected to learn to read at a tender age. When Charles, later Duc de Berry, was eight years old, he had a library of five books: an *ABC*, a copy of *Seven Penitential Psalms*, Cato's *Moral Sayings* and two Latin grammars. In wealthy families, the education of young children was left to mothers and domestic priests. But for others there were chantry schools which provided an elementary education. Older children were more formally educated in grammar schools, attached to cathedrals, run by city councils or founded by merchants.

A UNIVERSITY EDUCATION

Universities were the main sources of new ideas, many of which challenged the Church's traditional teaching. By 1500 there were 20 universities in Italy, 18 in France, 16 in Germany, 14 in Spain and Portugal, three in Scotland, and two in England.

The main subjects taught were civil and canon law, theology, medicine, metaphysics, philosophy, rhetoric and logic, and what was called the *quadrivium* – arithmetic, geometry, astronomy and music. Instruction was by lecture only, and courses were long – four years for a first degree, a further three years for an MA, and a further ten years for a doctorate. A great number of students dropped out in the first couple of years. The purpose of a university was to train young clerics, but many students had no wish to enter the Church. These young men would study composition, conveyancing, the drawing of wills, the keeping of accounts and legal pleading under a private tutor at Oxford, Paris or Padua for a few months, and then leave when it suited them.

The texts and books that formed the core of university courses changed little over the centuries. In 1500, students were using dictionaries and books that were written centuries before. Study of logic and metaphysics was still based on the writings of

---

EYEWITNESS

RULES FOR CONDUCT AT SCHOOL

❦... If anyone who knows Latin dares to speak English or French with his companion, or with any clerk, for every word he shall have a blow with the rod.

Likewise, for rudeness in word or deed anywhere and for any kind of oath let not the rod be spared; but let them use these words as their oath:

"Surely", "Of a truth", "Indeed", "I assure you", "No doubt", "God knows".

For any kind of falsehood anyone will be disciplined.

... Again, whoever at bedtime has torn to pieces the bed of his companions, or hidden the bedclothes, or thrown shoes or pillows from corner

to corner, or roused anger, or thrown the school into disorder, shall be severely punished in the morning.

In going to bed let them conduct themselves as upon rising, signing themselves and their beds with the sign of the cross ...❧

Anonymous manuscripts, 13th century

TEACHERS AND PUPILS A late medieval manuscript (above) shows a tutor with his students. In Lombardy, a servant gently fans the young Prince Maximilian Sforza (right) as he attends his lessons.

Aristotle, just as the study of medicine was based on the works of Galen, who had lived in the 2nd century AD. The popular appeal of a university depended almost entirely on its teachers and lecturers.

Teachers did all they could to discourage competition, especially from former pupils. For example, laws were brought in to restrict the supply of new teachers at the University of Paris in 1215: 'No one shall lecture in the arts at Paris before he is 21 years of age and he shall have heard lectures for at least six years before he begins to lecture ...' Furthermore, no one under the age of 35 was allowed to lecture in theology.

There was no corporal punishment at medieval universities, though the students were commonly regarded as wild, unruly and violent. First-year undergraduates, or freshmen, were often known as *bajans* – from the French *bec jaune*, literally 'yellow beak', a reference to fledgling birds – and they frequently had

CODE OF CONDUCT
The popular school-book *Cato* was a series of Latin verses on civilised behaviour.

to go through elaborate initiation ceremonies. In France, a *bajan* had to stand with his head uncovered to receive a blow on the scalp with a ferrule. If the poor student made any sound, he received two more blows. After his first year, the French *bajan* was purged of his wildness by a ceremonial washing in public, after which he was led through the streets of the city on an ass. In Germany, the *bajan* was treated like a wild animal. His fellow students surrounded him, armed with augers, saws and pincers, to 'remove' imaginary horns, tusks and claws. It is hardly surprising, then, that many young students were seriously injured in the process.

As Latin was the only language formally taught for most of the Middle Ages, other languages had little or no commonly practised grammar or syntax. The French language spoken and written in Paris – and by the English upper classes from the Norman Conquest in 1066 until the middle of the 13th century – differed considerably from that of Marseilles or Bordeaux. Indeed, in the epics and fables of French literature, there emerged not one language, but two – the *langue d'oil* of the north and the *langue d'oc* of the

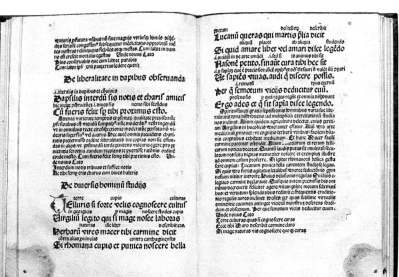

HANDWRITING A 15th-century scribe is surrounded by his books and tools.

LITERACY AND PRINTING

An exiled German goldsmith perfected the printing press.

It revolutionised learning, but brought its inventor to bankruptcy.

AROUND 1453 JOHANN GUTENBERG of Mainz produced his '42-line' Bible, the first document printed with movable metal type. Printing had existed in China for hundreds of years, but Gutenberg's achievement was a breakthrough for Europe and coincided with the increased manufacture of paper. In the centuries preceding Gutenberg's printing press,

BOOK OF HOURS This lavishly illuminated devotional book of prayers and readings was written and decorated in the 15th century for a Breton lady.

B FOR BLESSED Illuminated letters adorn the Winchester Bible.

professional scribes (several thousand in Paris alone) had found it increasingly hard to meet the demand for famous texts – causing the cultivated classes to complain bitterly about the copyists' delays.

Within a single generation printing presses were installed in every European country and city state. In 1464 a press was built in Rome by two Germans. By 1471 there were presses in Rome, Paris, Milan, Naples and Florence. By 1500 there were over 150 presses in Venice alone. William Caxton learnt how to build a press in Cologne in the early 1470s, and set up his own press in Westminster in 1476. Long before the end of the 15th century he had printed *The Canterbury Tales*, Malory's *Le Morte d'Arthur* and Aesop's *Fables*.

Early printed editions ran to only a few hundred copies, but it was the speed with which they could be reproduced and reprinted that mattered. Before the printing press, every copy of every book had to be hand-written, a laborious process that required great skill and hours of finger-cramping work with brush or quill pen. In the 50 years that

PRINT WORKSHOP Gutenberg invented the original printing press with movable type in the mid-15th century.

followed Gutenberg's invention over 100 different editions of the Bible were printed – 10,000 or more copies in all. By the end of the 15th century, well over 9 million books had been printed – a feat that all the skilled monks of medieval Europe could never have achieved.

FIRST ENGLISH PRINTER
This illustration in Caxton's first book is believed to show Caxton himself.

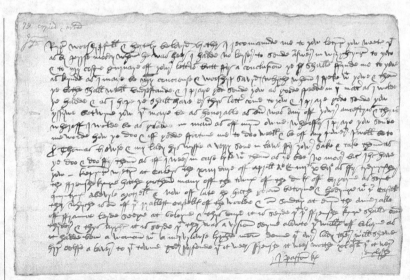

A LETTER HOME In a letter dated 1477, the young John Paston of Norfolk writes about his marriage and an anecdote from the French wars.

south. Similarly, in Spain, the different spoken languages included Catalan and Castilian, though the written tradition for much of the Middle Ages was Hebrew or Arabic.

Latin continued to be used for serious literature and in the professions. In addition, writers such as Dante, Petrarch and Chaucer were seen as revolutionaries in that they wrote in their native languages, making literature accessible to their countrymen. Their works were popular for another reason – they wrote about contemporary events and people living at that time. Chaucer's *The Canterbury Tales* delighted its first readers because they recognised the characters and events of which he wrote. The increasing use by writers of the English, French, Italian and Spanish vernacular strengthened national identities in the emerging states of Europe. It also challenged the Church's restrictions on the free exchange of new ideas.

STUDYING TEXTS
A 14th-century master instructs his pupils (above). A student distributes library books at the Ave Maria College in Paris (left).

LANGUAGE AND LITERATURE
The growth of literacy in English during the 15th century had produced a rapidly increasing demand for books, including translations from Latin and French. The most sumptuous manuscripts were specially commissioned by wealthy patrons as possessions of beauty to go with their tapestries and plate, but the vast majority of books were bought to read. Books of devotion and guides to heraldry, etiquette, the law and languages were popular, just as technical manuals are today, while romance, history and poetry were read for pleasure by the upper and middle classes.

The old oral tradition of minstrels, troubadours and balladeers persisted throughout Europe – men who wandered from place to place, reciting deeds of heroism or stories of saints and martyrs in verse form. More and more writers, however, turned to prose, producing several of the most famous works of the Middle Ages – Froissart's *Chronicles* and Boccaccio's *Decameron* among them.

THE DAWN OF THE RENAISSANCE
Medieval codes of behaviour and ways of thought were shaken beyond recovery by new ideas in art and morality that originated in Florence and slowly spread through Europe in the 15th century. These ideas included the belief that the study of man was as worthwhile as the study of God; that it was virtuous to lead a life of action in the world; that the possession of wealth was not necessarily a bad thing; that the

---

DID YOU KNOW?

Arabic numerals (1,2,3,4,5, and so on) were not introduced into Europe until the beginning of the 13th century. Roman numerals were used for all numbering and accounting until Gerbert of Rheims brought the new system to France in 1202. Even then, the system was incomplete and fraught with difficulty, for there was no medieval symbol for 'zero', so '27' and '207' looked the same.

artist should concern himself with the real world; that the life of a monk was not unquestionably superior to the life of an ordinary citizen; and that literature and art could serve as guides of how life should be lived.

The Renaissance rediscovery of Roman and Greek art, literature and philosophy was slow to spread. Florence was a republic (as ancient Rome and Athens had been), surrounded by rival and enemy cities, and the ideas seemed impious and revolutionary at first. Such thoughts challenged the Church's monopoly. No longer would the bookish cleric or cardinal be the sole arbiter of right and wrong. No longer would priest and prelate alone create the rules for art and architecture. No longer would faith itself be unquestioning and unquestionable.

THE AGE OF THE PATRON

With the Renaissance came the age of the great patron. Kings and queens, dukes and counts, popes and emperors, archbishops and rich merchants all liked to flaunt their wealth and power. They entertained their guests with ostentatious banquets; the magnificence of the livery worn by their servants, and the very size and appointments of their dwellings displayed that they were men of substance. But they also patronised the arts. The greatest works of medieval painters, poets, sculptors, architects and scholars were all commissioned by such men as Philip the Bold of Burgundy and the Duc de Berry in the 14th and 15th centuries. The Duc de Berry was responsible for 20 exquisitely illuminated, or painted, Books of Hours.

Italian businessmen patronised the arts all over Europe, especially in the Low Countries, where they found Flemish paintings that were both deeply religious and beautifully executed. The Burgundian John the Fearless, son of Philip the Bold, was the patron of Jan van Eyck, an artist regarded as the inventor of modern oil painting. The Medici family, though often guilty of appalling crimes and morals, commissioned the greatest of Italian writers to translate the works of Plato and Aristotle into Latin, and showered money on buildings and possessions.

Artists sought out patrons. When the young Leonardo da Vinci was interviewed by Ludovico Sforza of Milan in 1483, he appeared as a musician, knowing that Ludovico preferred music to painting. Later, when Leonardo applied for the post of city planner in Milan – under the same patron – he stressed that he was painter, architect, philosopher, poet, composer, sculptor, athlete, mathematician, inventor and anatomist. What mattered, however, was that Leonardo's political views were compatible with those of Ludovico.

Politics were often a hindrance. Most artists preferred to work for a king, an emperor or an archbishop. With a city council as patron, there was always the risk that control of the council would change hands, and consequently that support for a commissioned work or even for the artist himself would be suddenly withdrawn. When this happened, an artist would have to seek another patron. Giotto, for example, 'painted for many lords'; and Josquin des Pres, the great medieval composer, worked for the Pope, the King of France and the Holy Roman Emperor in turn.

EYEWITNESS

'OVER-TUNICS, TOGAS AND HOODS MAY BE WORN'

'Decency of garb' at the University of Paris:

❝ Artists go forth in black and round copes of noble brunet [a cloth made of dyed wool] ... or blue cloth lined with fur. Medical students wear copes the colour of thick rouge. Jurists wear scarlet. The reverend masters of theology, if regular clergy, are clad in the copes of their Order; if they are seculars, in any simple garb of humble colour ... Open over-tunics, togas and hoods may be worn by students when not attend-ing academic functions or when eating outside their own lodgings. Sleeveless vests – woollen close-fitting undergarments – may not be worn ... If anyone wishes to go on horseback or for exercise, he may wear what he pleases ...❞

Anonymous manuscript, 13th century

TIME CHART

NEWS OF THE WORLD

900 The Norseman Gunbjorn discovers Greenland after his ship is blown off course on a trip to Iceland.

901 Alfred the Great's son, Edward the Elder, becomes King of the Angles and Saxons.

924 Edward the Elder dies and is succeeded by his son, Athelstan, who will reign for 16 years until replaced by Eadwig.

960 Mieszko I of the house of Piast becomes the first ruler of the fledgling nation of Poland.

976 The foundations for the future Austria are laid when the Holy Roman Emperor, Otto II, grants the Franconian count Leopold land near the Danube.

978 Al-Mansur, the regent of Cordoba, assumes power in Muslim Spain and spreads the Omayyad caliphate northwards into the Christian kingdoms of the Iberian Peninsula.

985 Sweyn Forkbeard ascends the Danish throne (during his 30-year reign, he will conquer England and defeat both the Norwegians and Swedes).

987 Louis V of the Franks dies, ending the Carolingian Dynasty established by Charlemagne in 800. Hugh Capet founds a dynasty that will rule until 1328.

ROYAL HOMAGE King Athelstan presents St Cuthbert with a copy of *The Life of St Cuthbert*.

LEISURE AND LEARNING

925 The dialogue of *The Three Maries and the Angels*, the forerunner of the Easter Play, was first performed.

942 Arabs introduce kettledrums and trumpets to European culture.

950 Libraries, medical schools, a university and a thriving paper trade make the Muslim city of Cordoba the intellectual centre of Europe.

970 *The Exeter Book*, a collection of old English poetry, is compiled.

975 The modern system of arithmetical notation (1, 2, 3, 4, 5, and so on) is introduced by Arab mathematicians – it does not reach

western Europe until the early 13th century.

976 Construction begins on the Cathedral of St Mark, Venice.

980 An organ with 400 pipes is installed at a monastery in Winchester.

990 A method of systematic notation is developed for writing down music.

LOVE SONGS Troubadours entertain the courts of Europe.

LIFESTYLE CHANGES

PEPPER AND SPICE New trade routes bring increased supplies of spices from the East. They are kept in bowls and jars.

900 Smallpox is identified as a disease distinct from measles by Rhazes, the chief physician at a Baghdad hospital.

Medical school established at Salerno, Italy.

915 The Iberian Peninsula is hit by famine.

927 Famine sweeps through the Byzantine Empire.

942 The Flanders textile trade manufactures linen and woollen material.

943 Around 40,000 people in Limoges, France, die from ergotism, a disease caught after eating rust-contaminated rye.

962 A hospice is founded at St Bernard's Pass, Switzerland, for the use of travellers.

973 Spices, such as ginger, pepper and cloves, are imported from the East and go on sale in the markets of Mainz in Germany.

974 Authentic record of earthquake in Britain.

993 The first formal canonisation of saints takes place.

996 Sugar cane is first imported into Venice from Egypt.

11th CENTURY

1000 Lief Ericson, son of Norseman Eric the Red, discovers a land where 'grapes' grow – he calls it Vinland – but is unaware that he has set foot on a continent that will one day be called North America.

1016 Ethelred's death precipitates a conflict over succession – Londoners choose his son Edmund Ironside, while a *witan* (council) at Southampton prefers Sweyn Forkbeard's son, Canute. Edmund soon dies, leaving Canute to rule all England.

1042 Edward the Confessor, the last Anglo-Saxon king of England to reign his full course, ascends the throne.

1066 Edward the Confessor dies and is

CRUSADING SPIRIT The First Crusade sets sail.

COINAGE King Canute rules Denmark and England.

succeeded by Harold of Wessex, who is killed by the Normans at the Battle of Hastings, leaving William, Duke of Normandy to take the throne.

1096 After an appeal from Pope Urban, more than 30,000 men converge on Constantinople and, with the backing of the Byzantine emperor, set out for the Holy Land on the First Crusade.

1099 Jerusalem falls to the Crusaders, who massacre 40,000 inhabitants and burn synagogues and mosques.

NEWS OF THE WORLD

1000 The first recorded manuscript of *Beowulf*, a heroic poem composed in Old English, is written down.

1015 Work begins on Strasbourg Cathedral in Germany.

1025 Do, re, mi, fa, so, la, ti, do – the Benedictine monk Guido d'Arezzo introduces 'solmisation' to music. (In 1036, he pioneers modern musical notation.)

1050 The *Mabinogion*, a collection of Welsh tales, is compiled.

1052 King Edward the Confessor orders the construction of Westminster Abbey in London.

1067 In England, work begins on the Bayeux Tapestry around this date. It depicts the defeat of King Harold by William the Conqueror.

1078 William I begins the construction of the Tower of London.

1087 St Paul's Cathedral, London, is burned down and work starts on rebuilding.

1090 Gondolas make their appearance along the waterways of Venice.

A GREAT FIRE Rebuilding begins on St Paul's, London, following a devastating fire.

LEISURE AND LEARNING

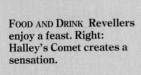

FOOD AND DRINK Revellers enjoy a feast. Right: Halley's Comet creates a sensation.

1000 Fear of Judgment Day spreads across Europe as the 1st millennium of the Christian era comes to an end.

The Chinese are said to have perfected gunpowder, a mixture of potassium nitrate, sulphur and charcoal.

1021 Europe suffers epidemics of St Vitus' dance, a form of chorea named after a Christian martyr of the 3rd century AD.

1066 A comet illuminates the skies (it will be named Halley's Comet in 1705).

1071 Constantine the African, a physician who has studied at Babylon, brings Greek, Roman, Jewish and Arabian medical knowledge to western Europe with his translation of ancient texts into Latin at the monastery in Monte Cassino, Italy.

1080 Benedictine monasteries in Salerno, about 125 miles from Monte Cassino, encourage clerics and some women physicians to study medicine and to start compiling the first medieval list of medicinal drugs.

Lady Godiva, wife of Leofric, Earl of Mercia, dies around this date. She will be remembered for the probably mythical episode when the people of Coventry are said to have stayed indoors with their windows shut as she rode naked through the streets; her husband had promised to abolish his harsh taxes if she exposed herself in this way.

1090 The first water-driven mechanical clock is said to have been invented in Peking.

LIFESTYLE CHANGES

12th CENTURY

NEWS OF THE WORLD

1120 After several years of fighting, Henry I of England makes peace with Louis VI of France but Henry's only legitimate heir is drowned in the White Ship disaster off Harfleur, France.

1135 Henry I of England dies and is succeeded by his nephew, Stephen of Boulogne.

1139 Matilda, Henry I's daughter, asserts her right to the English throne and lands at Arundel. In 1141, Stephen is captured and Matilda is proclaimed queen at Winchester; Stephen is eventually released and Matilda is forced to leave the country in 1147.

1151 Records show that the Chinese use explosives in war.

1170 Following his quarrel with Henry II and six years of exile in France, the Archbishop of Canterbury, Thomas Becket, is murdered by four knights in Canterbury Cathedral.

1189 Henry II of England dies and is succeeded by his son, Richard the Lionheart. His coronation is marked by a massacre of English Jews.

The Holy Roman Emperor, Frederick Barbarossa, leads the Third Crusade to the Holy Land but is drowned in the River Calycadnus in Cilicia, in the south of modern Turkey, the following year.

POWER PLAY The pope blesses Emperor Frederick Barbarossa.

LEISURE AND LEARNING

1100 The *Chanson de Roland*, an epic French poem of war and treachery, is composed around this date.

1123 The death of Omar Khayyam, the Persian poet and philosopher renowned for his *Rubaiyat*.

1125 Troubadour and trouvère music

become a feature of everyday life in southern France.

1136 Early examples of Gothic architecture can be seen in the pointed arches and high clerestory windows of the Church of St Denis in France.

1150 Paris University is founded.

The oldest book in Welsh, *The Black Book of Carmarthen*, is written down.

1155 Chess is played in England for the first time around this date.

1162 The French begin the construction of Notre Dame Cathedral in Paris (completed in 1235).

DEATH OF A LEGEND Excalibur is returned to the lake as Arthur dies.

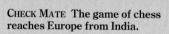

CHECK MATE The game of chess reaches Europe from India.

1167 Oxford University is founded.

1170 Chrétien de Troyes writes *Lancelot*, a tale of courtly love.

The legends of King Arthur are assembled by the Anglo-Latin poet Walter Map.

1191 The cycle of tales known as the *Nibelungenlied* is first recorded in Germany (to be completed by 1204).

LIFESTYLE CHANGES

1104 The volcano of Mount Hekla in Iceland, later known as the entrance to Hell, erupts, devastating a large area of farmland.

1120 Anglo-Saxon scientist Walcher of Malvern measures latitude and longitude in degrees, minutes and seconds.

1128 Cistercian monks from Normandy embark upon a programme of reclaiming swamps, and breeding cattle and horses, from which English agriculture will benefit.

1148 Crusaders returning from the Levant bring sugar back to Europe, where it is almost unknown.

1151 Henry II's wife, Eleanor of Aquitaine, introduces cheap wines into

England from France for the first time.

1180 The owners of some private houses in England use glass in their windows around this date.

Windmills with vertical sails are erected in parts of Europe.

1190 Paper is produced at the first paper mill in Christian Europe, built at Herault, France.

Ye Olde Trip to Jerusalem opens in Nottingham; one day it will be the oldest pub in England.

1190 The English import indigo from India for dyeing textiles.

1193 The first recorded merchant guild is founded in London.

BETTER YIELDS A Cistercian monk tends the crops. Below: better ploughs mean improved yields.

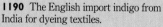

13th CENTURY

CROWNING GLORY **The coronation of Louis VIII of France.**

1204 Crusaders take Constantinople, and establish a Latin empire with Baldwin IX, Count of Flanders, as its first emperor. (The empire ends in 1261 when a Greek army restores Byzantine control to Constantinople.)

1212 King Alphonso VIII of Castile ends the Moorish domination of much of the Iberian peninsula.

1215 King John of England grants his subjects a Great Charter (Magna Carta), restricting his rights to tax arbitrarily.

1216 Following his conquest of China, Genghis Khan ravages much of the Near East with his 60,000 Mongol horsemen.

1241 The Hanseatic League is formed

by trading towns on the Baltic Sea; their ships introduce new technological advances, such as the rudder and the bowsprit.

1258 English barons seek to use Parliament as a means to control Henry III.

1271 The Venetian merchant Marco Polo sets out on his travels to China from where he will return in 1295.

1278 The Count of Hapsburg assumes the sovereignty of Austria, beginning a dynasty that will last for 640 years.

1290 The Ottoman Empire is founded by the King of Bythnia, Osman al-Ghazi, when he sets up the Muslim principality of Osmanli.

1200 Cymbals are introduced as musical instruments to Europe.

Engagement rings come into fashion in Europe around this date.

1203 *Parzival,* an epic German romance based on the story of the Holy Grail, is written by poet Wolfram von Eschenbach.

1210 *Tristan und Isolde* is written by Gottfried von Strassburg.

1217 Cambridge University is founded.

1218 Denmark adopts the Danneborg, which will become the oldest national flag in the world.

1220 Work begins on Salisbury Cathedral.

COLOUR AND LIGHT **Stained glass is used in Europe's cathedrals.**

1220 Giraffes are exhibited as curiosities in Europe.

1222 In honour of England's patron saint, April 23 becomes St George's Day and a national holiday.

1225 *Sumer is icumen in,* the earliest surviving English round song (a song with a recurring refrain), is composed by an anonymous writer.

The *Roman de la Rose,* an allegory of courtly love and chivalry, appears in France and will become one of the most popular of medieval poems.

1260 After 66 years of construction, Chartres Cathedral in France is consecrated.

1285 *Lohengrin,* an epic German poem, is written anonymously.

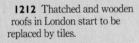

1212 Thatched and wooden roofs in London start to be replaced by tiles.

1225 Cotton is manufactured in Spain around this time.

1230 Crusaders returning from the Holy Land bring leprosy to England.

1233 Coal is mined in Newcastle, England, for the first time.

1253 Linen is manufactured in England.

1265 Monks from St Peter's Abbey set up a fruit and vegetable stall in

EYE GLASSES **Spectacles are mentioned in an Italian treatise.**

what will become Covent Garden in London.

1269 England's first toll roads are established.

1278 Coin clippers, or counterfeiters, in London face a crackdown from the authorities, but the punishment depends on religion – 278 Jews are hanged while Christians are simply fined.

1289 The first record of spectacles, invented around 1287, comes from Sandro di Popozo : 'I am so debilitated by age that without the glasses known as spectacles, I would no longer be able to read or write.'

1298 The introduction of the spinning wheel revolutionises the textile industry.

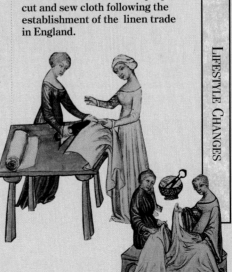

TEXTILE TRADE **Workers prepare, cut and sew cloth following the establishment of the linen trade in England.**

14th CENTURY

NEWS OF THE WORLD

1306 France and England expel large numbers of Jews.

1314 Robert Bruce leads 30,000 Scotsmen to victory over 100,000 Englishmen at the Battle of Bannockburn, taking Stirling Castle and securing Scottish independence.

1337 England and France embark upon a Hundred Years' War, after England claims French territories such as Normandy and

SCOTTISH HERO Robert the Bruce secures Scottish independence.

Anjou, and Edward III declares himself King of France.

1346 England inflicts a mighty defeat on France at the Battle of Crécy. (In 1356, the French suffer another defeat at Poitiers.)

1368 The Ming emperor Hongwu (Hung-wu) orders the rebuilding of the Great Wall of China.

1369 Tamerlane becomes ruler of Samarkand and begins to assemble a mighty army that will set out to conquer the world.

1377 Edward III of England dies and is succeeded by his grandson Richard II, whose father was the Black Prince.

1378 Reforms initiated by Pope Urban VI incense many cardinals who install Robert of Geneva as Pope Clement VII at Avignon, thus creating a Great Schism that splits the Catholic Church.

FIGHTING METHODS English and French soldiers clash at the Battle of Crécy

LEISURE AND LEARNING

1305 The Italian painter Giotto di Bondone creates such masterpieces as the fresco cycle *Lives of the Virgin and*

Christ on the walls of Padua's Church of Santa Maria dell' Arena. His new realistic style will influence the great masters of the Renaissance.

1307 The Italian poet Dante Alighieri begins one of the great works of medieval literature – *La Divina Commedia,* an imaginary journey through hell, purgatory and paradise.

1311 Notre Dame Cathedral at Rheims, a masterpiece of Gothic architecture, is completed after almost a century of construction.

IMITATING LIFE Giotto introduces a new sense of realism into art.

1314 St Paul's Cathedral in London is completed.

1345 The Cathedral of Notre Dame is finished on the Ile de la Cité in Paris – it has taken 182 years to complete.

1353 The Italian humanist Giovanni Boccaccio completes his *Decameron,* a collection of earthy tales set against the background of the Black Death that has ravaged Europe.

1387 English poet Geoffrey Chaucer writes the tragic love story *Troilus and Criseyde* and begins work on *The Canterbury Tales.*

1392 Jacques Gringonneur, painter at the court of Charles VI of France, designs the deck of playing cards (52 cards, four suits) that will survive until the present day.

LIFESTYLE CHANGES

1303 A merchants' charter is granted by England's Edward I, giving foreign merchants free access to the country's markets and allowing them to leave with any goods they have bought or been unable to sell (except wine).

1305 Edward I of England standardises the yard and the acre as measures of distance and area respectively.

1306 A citizen is found guilty of burning coal in London, a capital offence, and is executed.

1315 The Italian surgeon Mondino de Luzzi systematically dissects a human cadaver in public – an act that has been forbidden for centuries.

Famine sweeps across western Europe.

1320 The monastic monopoly of manuscripts and other forms of written communication is broken after paper produced at Mainz – and shortly afterwards at Augsburg, Cologne and Nuremberg – starts to replace vellum.

1332 Oranges, hitherto unknown in Europe, go on sale in Nice, France.

1337 The first scientific weather forecasts are produced by William Merlee of Oxford, England.

1348 The Black Death, which originated in China in 1333, spreads to Florence, Paris and London. The disease is widely blamed on the Jews, who are fiercely persecuted, particularly in Germany. Around a third of the population of England will die.

1375 The Hanseatic League of some 70 north European cities is recognised by the Holy Roman Emperor, and establishes a system of weights, measures and coinage.

1379 William of Wykeham establishes Winchester College, one of England's public schools.

MEDICINE Dissections are allowed for the study of anatomy.

15th CENTURY

1413 Henry IV of England dies and is succeeded by his son, Henry V.

1415 The English inflict a massive defeat on the French at the Battle of Agincourt, enabling Henry V to take Normandy.

1422 Henry V of England dies of dysentery in France and is succeeded by his eight-month-old son, Henry VI. After the death of Charles VI of France, Henry VI is proclaimed King of France, too.

1429 Joan of Arc liberates Orleans from the English siege and persuades the dauphin that he is legitimately King of France – he is crowned Charles VII.

1452 The German, Frederick IV, is the

last Holy Roman Emperor to be crowned at Rome.

1453 The Ottoman Turks take Constantinople and end almost 1000 years of rule by the Byzantine Empire. The imposition of tariffs by the Turks eventually spurs European traders to seek new routes to the East.

The Hundred Years' War between England and France comes to an end as the English leave every corner of France except Calais.

1455 In England the Wars of the Roses break out between the houses of Lancaster and York.

1485 Henry, Earl of Richmond, defeats and kills Richard III at the Battle of

Bosworth, and founds the Tudor monarchy as Henry VII.

1492 The Genoese seafarer Christopher Columbus sets sail in an attempt to find a westward route to Cathay. He lands in the Bahamas, thinking he has reached the East Indies.

AT THE STAKE Joan of Arc prepares to die.

1415 Three Belgian brothers, Pol, Herman and Jan Limburg, produce *Les Très Riches Heure du duc de Berry*.

1434 Jan van Eyck paints *The Arnolfini Marriage*.

1456 The German Johann Gutenburg prints the Gutenburg Bible at Mainz on a press that uses movable type.

1466 In Bruges, Belgium, the English

DAILY LIFE A scene from *Les Très Riches Heures*.

printer William Caxton publishes the first book printed in English – *The Recuyell of the Historyes of Troye*. (In 1476 he establishes the first English print shop in London.)

1470 York Minster – dedicated to St Peter – is completed after 250 years.

1475 Winchester Cathedral is completed.

1489 The mathematical symbols plus (+) and minus (–) are used for the first time, in John Widman's *Mercantile Arithmetic*.

ARTIST'S STUDIO A woman artist works on a painting of the Virgin and Child while an apprentice grinds the pigment.

1497 *The Last Supper* by the Florentine painter Leonardo da Vinci is unveiled in Milan.

1403 To combat the spread of the bubonic plague, a quarantine of 40 days is imposed by the doge of Venice on anyone wishing to enter the city.

1429 The Grocers' Company is formed in London; it is allowed to sell goods wholesale and to coordinate trade in drugs, dyes and spices.

1440 The King's College of Our Lady of Eton (Eton College) is founded near Windsor Castle.

1441 Africans from the region near Cape Blanc in West Africa are sold by Portuguese traders in the markets of Lisbon, so beginning a black slave trade in which an estimated 20 million Africans will eventually be shipped to Europe and the New World.

1456 Sugar grown in Madeira is shipped to Bristol, sweetening the palate of many an Englishman for the first time.

1464 The first national postal service is the Poste Royale in France.

1471 Brussels takes over from Arras as the centre of the tapestry industry in Europe.

1489 An epidemic of typhus strikes Europe for the first time – after Spanish soldiers bring the disease back to Aragon from Cyprus.

1494 A lottery is established in Germany.

1495 The first recorded outbreak of syphilis occurs in Naples.

HEALTH SERVICE Secular hospitals are set up following the large numbers of deaths caused by diseases such as bubonic plague.

ACKNOWLEDGMENTS

ABBREVIATIONS: T = Top; M = Middle; B = Bottom; R = Right; L = Left.

1 *Luttrell Psalter*, 1335-40, Add. MS. 42130, f.171 / British Library, London. **2-3** *Histoires Romaines de Jean Mansel*, 15th century, MS. 5087, f.144v / Bibliothèque de l'Arsenal, Paris. **4** *Historia Naturalis*, Sienese c.1460, (detail) Victoria & Albert Museum, London / E.T. Archive, T; *Luttrell Psalter*, 1335-40, Add. MS. 42130, ff.181v-182 / British Library, London, M; *Guillaume de Machaut*, Sienese 14th century / E.T. Archive, MR; Bibliothèque Nationale, Paris, B. **5** *Barthélémy l'Anglais: Livre de la Propriété des Choses*, Bibliothèque Nationale, Paris T; *15th century Medical Treatise*, Bibliothèque Nationale, Paris / Bridgeman Art Library, London, ML; *Historia Naturalis*, Sienese c.1460, (detail) Victoria & Albert Museum, London / E.T. Archive, MR; *Luttrell Psalter*, 1335-40, Add. MS. 42130, f.170v / British Library, London, B. **7** Bibliothèque Nationale, Paris / E.T. Archive. **8** Cott. Dom. AXV11, f.177v / British Library, London, BL; *Ellesmere Chaucer*, facsimile, Victoria & Albert Museum, London / E.T. Archive. **9** Harley MS. 4431, f.150, 15th century / British Library, London / Bridgeman Art Library, London, T; Biblioteca Marciana, Venice, 14th century / E.T. Archive, MR; *Great Domesday Book*, facsimile / Editions Alecto Limited, B. **10** *Robinet Testard: François I and Marguerite d'Angoulême playing chess*, 15th century, Bibliothèque Municipale, Paris, TL; Bibliothèque Municipale, Rouen / Lauros-Giraudon. **11** *Livres des Prouffits Champêtres*, MS. 5064, f.1. **12** Victoria & Albert Museum, London / Bridgeman Art Library, London. **13** *Jean Bourdichon: The Four Conditions of Society: Nobility*, (detail) Ecole des Beaux Arts, Paris / Giraudon /Bridgeman Art Library, London. **14** *Andrea Mantegna: Famiglia e corte di Ludovico III Gonzaga, Palazzo Ducale, Mantua* / Scala. **15** MS. 5073 f.117v Fr. 15th century, Bibliothèque de l'Arsenal, Paris / Giraudon / Bridgeman Art Library, London, ML; *Arthur Lockwood*, BL; *Flemish Parade Shield*, 15th century / Michael Holford, BR. **16** *Le Rustican*, 15th century, MS. 340/603, Musée Conde, Chantilly / Lauros-Giraudon / Bridgeman Art Library, London, TL; Harley MS. 4425, f. 12, British Library, London / Bridgeman Art Library, London, BR. **17** *Miniatures from Minnesänger Manuscript*, German, c 1300 / Heidelberg University, TL; *The Book of the Heart Possessed by Love by René of Anjou*, 15th century /Österreichische Nationalbibliothek, Vienna, B. **18** *Luttrell Psalter*, 1335-40, Add. MS. 42130, f.60, British Library, London / Bridgeman Art Library, London, T; *Hours of May of Burgundy, Flanders c.1477*, (detail) National Library of Vienna cod 1857 / E.T Archive, BL; **19** *Jan Van Eyck: The Arnolfini Marriage*, 1434, National Gallery, London / Bridgeman Art Library, London. **20** *Jean Auguste Dampt: Statue of Sire de Coucy, Plaque d'Enguerrand VII de Coucy, Histoire du chatelain de Coucy* / Giraudon. **21** Add. MS. 24098, January (detail) / British Library, London, TL; Drawing by Victor Ambrus, TR. **22** Museum of London, TL; MS. 15426, f.86, MS. 11695, f.86, (detail) MS. 18851, f.184 (detail), British Library, London / Robert Harding Picture Library, London, TR, BL, BR. **23** Michael Holford, T; *The Warwick Gittern*, English c.14th century, British Museum, London / Bridgeman Art Library, London, BL; *The Eton Choir Book*, Eton College, Windsor, BR. **24** Bodley 264, f.133v / Bodleian Library, Oxford, BL. **25** Bodley MS. 249, f.197, 15th century / British Library, London, T; Private Collection, B. **26** *Domenico di Bartolo: Marriage of the Foundlings*, (detail) Spedale di Santa Maria Della Scala, Siena, photo by F. Lensini / Bridgeman Art Library, London. **27** Michael Holford; Private Collection, TR. **28** *Aesop's Fables*, Bibliothèque Nationale, Paris / E.T. Archive, L. **28-29** Drawings by Victor Ambrus. **30** Add. MS. 24098, f.25b, British Library, London, T; Drawing by Victor Ambrus, BR. **31** MS. Bodley 264, f.123v (detail) The Bodleian Library, Oxford / Bridgeman Art Library, London. **32** *Luttrell Psalter*, 1335-40, Add. MS. 42130, f.196 / British Library, London, M; *Arithmetic Book* by Filippo Calandri, photo Laboratorio Fotografico Donato Pineider, Florence / From: *Europe 1492: Portrait of a Continent Five Hundred Years Ago* by Franco Cardini, published by Facts on File, 1989; Hunter MS. 100, f.52 / Arthur Lockwood. **33** Add. 19776, f.72v, British Library, London / Bridgeman Art Library, London. **34** *Sundial*, 1493, Strasbourg/Lauros-Giraudon, TR; *Motive Clock*, drawing by Dondi. c 1350, Land. MS. 620 / Bodleian Library, Oxford, ML; *Portable Sundial*, 10th century, Canterbury Cathedral/ Bridgeman Art Library, London, BR. **35** *Goddess Atemprance and Clock with Hanging Bells*, 15th century, MS. Bodley 421, f. 4v, TL; *14th century German Alarm Clock/* Mainfränkisches Museum, Würzburg, ML; *Astrological Clock, Clock Tower, St. Mark's Square, Venice/ Michael Holford, MR.* **36** *Hugo Van der Goes: The Poltinari Altarpiece*, (detail) Uffizi, Florence / Bridgeman Art Library, London,TL; Cott. Aug. A.V.103 / British Library, London, TR. **37** Add. MS 17012, f.2 / British Library, London.

38 E.T.Archive. **39** MS 5073 f.140v, 15th century, Bibliothèque de l'Arsenal, Paris. **40** *Limbourg Brothers: Les Très Riches Heures du Duc de Berry, September*, 15th century, Victoria & Albert Museum, London / Bridgeman Art Library, London. **41** E.T. Archive L; *The da Costa Hours*. MS. 399, f.2v, Flemish, c.1515/ The Pierpont Morgan Library, New York, R. **42-43** Drawing by Gill Tomblin. **44** *Barthélemy l'Anglais: Livre de la Propriété des Choses* / Bibliothèque Nationale, Paris. **45** Add. MS. 19720, f.165 / British Library, London, T; *Rogier Van der Weyden: Nativity c.1453* (detail) / Staatliche Museen Preussischer Kulturbesitz, Berlin BR. **46-47** Drawing by Gill Tomblin. **48** *Limbourg Brothers: Les Très Riches Heures du Duc de Berry*, (detail) 15th century, Victoria & Albert Museum, London / Bridgeman Art Library, London. **49** E.T. Archive; *Benninck Book of Hours, April*, Victoria & Albert Museum, London / Add. MS. 19720, f.117v, 15th century, British Library, London / Bridgeman Art Library, London, TR, BL. **50** *Portrait Bust of Hans von Burghausen/ Bildarchiv Foto Marburg*, TR; *Mason's Dividers*, York Minster / Angelo Hornak Library, TR; *Chartres Cathedral, South Choir*, 13th century/ Sonia Halliday, M; *Cologne Cathedral, The Nave Roof/* Angelo Hornak Library, B. **51** *Bourges Cathedral/* Scala, TL; *Durham Cathedral, the Nave/* Angelo Hornak Library, TR; *Duomo, Pisa/* Scala, B. **52** *Missel, de Martin de Beaune*, 15th century / Bibliothèque Nationale, Paris. **53** MS. Douce 374, f.17 / The Bodleian Library, Oxford; *Luttrell Psalter*, 1335-40, Add. MS. 42130, f.172b, British Library, London, BR; MS. Rawl Lit e.36, f.6v, The Bodleian Library, Oxford / Bridgeman Art Library, London, TL; *Assisa Paris*, 1266 / By Courtesy of the Corporation of London, M; *Tacuinum Sanitatis*. MS. s.n2644, f.82v, Italian, c.1385 / Österreichische Nationalbibliothek, Vienna, TR. **55** Ms. Rawl. G.98, f.49v, The Bodleian Library, Oxford / Bridgeman Art Library, London, T; *P. de Crescens: Le Rustican c.1460*, Musée Conde, Chantilly / Giraudon / Bridgeman Art Library, London. **56-57** Drawings by Victor Ambrus. **57** Museum of London, TL; E.T. Archive,TR; The Wallace Collection, B. **58** *Master Rogier de Salerne: A Book of Surgery* (detail) British Library, London / Bridgeman Art Library, London, T; Stowe MS. 955, f.7, (detail), British Library, London / Bridgeman Art Library, London,BR. **59** *Boccace de Claris Mulieribus: The Story of Gaia, Women in the Role of Men's Work* Fr.12420, f.71, Bibliothèque Nationale, Paris / Bridgeman Art Library, London TL; Stained Glass Roundel, Victoria & Albert Museum, London / Michael Holford,TR; *Blessed Clare Master: Vision of the Blessed Clare of Rimini*, c.1340, (detail) / The National Gallery, London, BL. **60** *The Garden of Medicinal Plants*, Bibliothèque Nationale, Paris / Bridgeman Art Library, London, TR; *Carlo Crivelli: The Annunciation, with Saint Emidius*, (detail) / The National Gallery, London, BL. **61** Royal MS. 15 E111, f.269, (detail), British Library, London / Bridgeman Art Library, London, TR. *Florentine School: Marriage Ceremony*, Victoria & Albert Museum, London, B. **62** Private Collection, TR; *Luttrell Psalter*, 1335-40, Add. MS. 42130, f.63 / British Library, London, BL. **63** *Rogier van der Weyden: Portrait of a Lady, c.1450* / The National Gallery, London / Bridgeman Art Library, London, TL; Sloane MS. 2435, f.8v, (detail) / British Library, London. **64** British Museum, London / Bridgeman Art Library, London, TL; Sloane MS. 2435, f.8v, (detail) / British Library, London. **65** *Hortus Sanitatis*, Mainz 1491 / Natural History Museum, London, TL; Drawing by Victor Ambrus, BR. **66** *Brueghel, the Elder: Peasant Wedding*, (detail) Kunsthistorisches Museum, Vienna / Bridgeman Art Library, London. **67** MS. Douce. 383, f.17 v, (detail), The Bodleian Library, Oxford, Bridgeman Art Library, London, T; *Stained Glass Roundel*, / Victoria & Albert Museum, MR. **68** British Library, London / Robert Harding Picture Library, London. **69** *Jean Bourdichon: The Four Conditions of Society: Industry*, (detail) Ecole des Beaux Arts, Paris / Bridgeman Art Library, London. **70** *Croissens Manual of Agriculture*, (detail) British Library, London / Bridgeman Art Library, London. **71** MS. Auct. D.2.6, f.6v / Bodleian Library, Oxford. **72** MS. 1044 (0-4) f.123, Bibliothèque de Rouen / Giraudon. **73** Add. MS. 24098, f.26v, British Library, London / Bridgeman Art Library, London, BL; *Luttrell Psalter*, 1335-40, Add. MS. 42130, f.173 / British Library, London, BR. **74-75** Drawings by Gill Tomblin.**76** Royal MS. 18E, f.175, British Library, London / Bridgeman Art Library, London, T; Kentish Peasant, f.337v Archbishop Coutenay's Register / Lambeth Palace, B. **77** Priors Hall Barn, Widdington / English Heritage. **78** Royal MS. 2BV111, f.155v, British Library, London / Bridgeman Art Library, London, MR; E.T. Archive BR. **79** *Luttrell Psalter*, 1335-40, Add. MS. 42130, f.158 / British Library, London, T; MS. Douce 93 f.28r (detail) / Bodleian Library, Oxford, B. **80** *P.de Crescens: Le Rustican* c.1460, Musée Conde, Chantilly / Bridgeman Art Library, London. **81** Michael Holford, T; *Luttrell Psalter*, 1335-40, Add. MS. 42130, f.173r MR. **82** *Tacuinum Sanitatis*, M.s.n2644, f.85v c.1385, Italian / Österreichische National-bibliothek, Vienna. **83** Hamburg Staatsarchiv / E.T. Archive TL; Drawing by Victor

Ambrus BR. **84** Collegio del Cambio Perugia / E.T. Archive TL; MS. 9066, Bibliothèque Royale, Brussels / Bridgeman Art Library, London, TR. **85** FR.9136, f.344, Bibliothèque Nationale, Paris / Bridgeman Art Library, London, B; British Museum, London MR. **86** Drawing by Victor Ambrus. **87** MS. 27695, f.8, (detail) British Library, London / Bridgeman Art Library, London, T; *Historia Naturalis, Sienese, c.1460*, Victoria & Albert Museum / E.T. Archive BL.**88** *Italian Inn*, 14th century/ Biblioteca Marciana, Venice/ Giraudon, T; *German Guesthouse*, 15th century/ German National Museum, Nürnberg/ Archiv Für Kunst Und Geschichte, Berlin, B. **89** *Drinking Scene*, fresco by Ghirlandaio, St. Martino dei Buonomini, Florence/ Scala.**90** Trinity College, Dublin BR. **91** Fr.MS. 247, f.153v, Bibliothèque Nationale, Paris / Bridgeman Art Library, London / E.T. Archive TL. **93** Sloane MS 2435, f.44v, (detail) British Library T; E.T. Archive (detail) B. **94** *Clermont: Livres des Passages d'Outremer*, 15th century / Sonia Halliday TL; Photo by Adam Woolfit / Robert Harding Picture Library, London, B. **95** FR.4276, f.6, FR.22495, f.235v, Bibliothèque Nationale, Paris / Bridgeman Art Library T, MR; *Luttrell Psalter*, 1335-40 Add. MS. 42130, f.82, British Library, London BR. **97** British Library, London T; Board of Trustees of the Royal Armouries BR. **98-99** Board of Trustees of the Royal Armouries. **100** Board of Trustees of the Royal Armouries T, MR,BL; Milanese Field Armour, Italian, 1445, Glasgow Museums: Art Gallery & Museum, Kelvingrove ML, Wallace Collection, London M, MS. Amb.317.2, f.10v, Stadtbibliothek, Nuremburg / Robert Harding Picture Library / Bridgeman B. **101** E.T. Archive. **102** E.T. Archive TR; *Luttrell Psalter*, 1335-40 Add.MS. 42130, f.56 / British Library, London ML. **103** Add.MS. 15269, f.178v/ British Library, London. **104** *Maciejowsky Bible c.1250*, Pierpont Morgan Library, New York. **105** Royal MS. 15E1, f.335 (detail) British Library, London. **106** E.T. Archive. **107** *Siege of Rhodes*, Latin, 15th century, Bibliothèque Nationale, Paris / Bridgeman Art Library, London. **108** *Mappamondo, Fra' Mauro*, Biblioteca Marciana/ Scala, TL; *Portolan Chart* by Angellino de Dalorto, 1339/ Royal Geographical Society, London, BR. **109** *Ptolemy from Cosmografia Ulm*, 1482/ National Historical Museum, Bucharest/ E.T. Archive, TM; *Islamic Astrolabe*, 1236, Egyptian/ British Museum, London/ Michael Holford, TM; *Ptolemaic Map of the World*, woodcut, 1486/ British Museum, London/ Michael Holford, TR; *Mappamondo Catalano/* Biblioteca Estense, Modena/ Scala, BL; *Globe*, Martin Behaim/ Archiv Für Kunst Und Geschichte, Berlin, BR. **111** Add. MS. 11353, f.9, British Library, London T; Royal MS. 10E IV, f.187, (detail) British Library, London / Bridgeman Art Library, London, MR. **113** *The Whaddon folio c1460- The Kings Bench*, Inner Temple / E.T. Archive TL; Fr.MS. 41, f.42v, Bibliothèque Municipale, AGEN / Bridgeman Art Library, London BR. **114-115** MS. Fr.2643, f.11, MS. Fr. 616, f.67, Bibliothèque Nationale, Paris / Bridgeman Art Library, London. **116** MS. 19D. III, f.266, British Library, London. **117** *Johan Fouquet: The Martyrdom of St Apollonia*, Fr71, f.39, Musée Condè, Chantilly / Giraudon / Bridgeman Art Library, London, T; Bodleian Library, Oxford, MR. **118-119** Drawings By Victor Ambrus. **120** Add. MS. 27695, f14 (detail) British Library, London ML; *Limbourg Brothers: Les Très Riches Heures du Duc de Berry*, (detail), Victoria & Albert Museum, London / Bridgeman Art Library, London, T; *Benninck Book of hours*, (detail) Victoria & Albert Museum, London / Bridgeman Art Library, London, BR. **121** MS. Latin 963, f.264, (detail) Bibliothèque Nationale, Paris, TL; *Playfair Book of Hours*, French 15th century (detail), Victoria & Albert Museum, London / E.T.Archive TR; *Limbourg Brothers: Les Très Riches Heures du Duc de Berry*, (detail), Musée Conde, Chantilly / Giraudon, M; *Hours of the Duchess of Burgundy c.1450*, MS. 76 /1362, f.12v, Musée Conde, Chantilly / Giraudon / Bridgeman Art Library, London, BR. **122** Robert Harding Picture Library, London. **123** *Limbourg Brothers: Les Très Riches Heures du Duc de Berry*, 5th century, Victoria & Albert Museum, London / Bridgeman Art Library, London, T. **125** MS. 65 / 1284, f.71v, Musée Conde, Chantilly / Giraudon / Bridgeman Art Library, London; MS. Bodl.264, f.83 R (detail) / Arthur Lockwood, MR; E.T. Archive BR. **126** Fr.396, f.66, Bibliothèque Nationale, Paris / Bridgeman Art Library, London, T; Trinity College, Cambridge MS. 0.1.20, f.264v / Arthur Lockwood. **127** Ash.1462, f.15v-16r, 12th century, Bodleian Library, Oxford / Bridgeman Art Library, London T; Bodley. MS. 360, f.26v, Bodleian Library, Oxford / Bridgeman Art Library, London BR. **128** Sloane MS. 2435, f.11v, British Library, London / Arthur Lockwood. **129** *Fresco from the Villa Issogna, Val d'Aosta: The Pharmacy*, 15th century, Giraudon / Bridgeman Art Library, London, T; Sloane MS. 6, f.175v, British Library, London, ML. **130** *Unicorn*, Royal. MS. 12 FX 111, f. 10v/ British Museum, London, TL; French 12th century, Souvigny/ Lauros-Giraudon, BR. **131** *Painting of S. Nicola da Bari* by Fabriano/Pinacoteca, Vatican/ Scala, TL; *Lion*, Royal

MS. 12 CX1X, f. 6/ British Library, London, MR; *Latin Bestiary*, 13th century, Harley. MS. 3244, ff, 58-9v/ British Museum, London, BL. **133** The Pierpont Morgan Library, New York / E.T. Archive, TR; *Plate from Block-Book c1450 'Ars Moriendi'*, Private Collection, M/ E.T. Archive,T; Glasgow Museums: The Burrell Collection, TL; Cott.Tib.Avii.90, (detail), British Library, London BR; Museum of London, B. **135** MS. 76, f.2 f.169r, Koninklijke Kabinet, The Hague / Bridgeman Art Library, London; MS. Bod. e.13.f.97 / Bodleian Library, Oxford. **136-137** Drawing by Gill Tomblin. **138** Drawing by Victor Ambrus. **139** Merton 319, f.41r/ Bodleian Library, Oxford, TL; *Nicolas Oresme:'On Philosophy' by Aristotle*, 15th century, Bibliothèque Nationale, Paris / Bridgeman Art Library, London, MR. **141** *Bedford Hours*, French 1423, March, August, September, November (details) / Bridgeman Art Library, London. **142** *The Turin Shroud*, 13th century / E.T. Archive, TR; *Reliquary Cross of Pope Urbain V*, Prague Cathedral / Giraudon, BL; *Reliquary Diptych*, 14th century// Victoria & Albert Museum, London / Michael Holford, BR.**143** Galleria Naz. d'Arte Antica, Rome/ Scala, TL; *Pilgrim at Becket's Tomb*, 13th century/ Trinity Chapel, Canterbury / Sonia Halliday, TR; *Gold Head of St. Eustace*, German, 13th century/ Bridgeman Art Library, London BL.**145** MS. 2167, f.13v, Biblioteca Trivulziana, Milan / Bridgeman Art Library, London TL; Archivo Municipal, Barcelona / Bridgeman Art Library, London, M; *Classical Schoolbook: Cato*, Eton College, Windsor, BR. **146** MS. Fr.9198, f.19 / Bibliothèque Nationale, Paris, TL; Initial letter B. from Winchester Bible / Bridgeman Art Library, London, TR; Pages from *Book of Hours of the Virgin*, French 15th century, Glasgow Museums: The Burrell Collection, BL. **147** Photo Eric Lessing / Magnum Photos Limited, T; *Engraved Frontispiece, Recueyll of the Histories of Troy, 1474*, (detail), Huntingdon Library / E.T. Archive, BL; *Paston Letters*: MS. LXXIX p.244, f.31 / 145 / British Library, London, BR. **148** Royal MS. 17E 111, f.209, (detail), British Library, London / Bridgeman Art Library, London, B; Archives Nationales, Paris. **150** *King Althelstan presenting Bede's Life of St, Cuthbert to the Saint*, c.c.c.c. MS. 183, f. 1v/ Cambridge, Corpus College, T; *Manesse Codex*, German 14th century, Heidelberg University Library/ E.T. Archive, M; *Livre des Merveilles*, Fr. 2810, f. 84/ Bibliothèque Nationale, Paris/ Bridgeman Art Library, London, BL; Museum of London (detail), BR. **151** *The First Crusade*, 12th century Fr. 22495, f. 21r/ Bibliothèque Nationale, Paris/ Bridgeman Art Library, London, TL; British Museum, London/ Michael Holford, TR; *London to Apulia*, Matthew Paris, 13th century, Royal, MS. 14. c. V11, f. 2/ British Library, London, MR; *Bayeux Tapestry*, Musée de Bayeux/ Giraudon, BL; *Bayeux Tapestry*, Musée de Bayeux/ Michael Holford, BR. **152** Codex Correr, 1.383, Museo Correr, Venice/ Bridgeman Art Library, London, T; *Roman de Lancelot*, Add. MS. 10294, F. 94/ British Library, London/ Bridgeman Art Library, London, ML; Bodleian Library, Oxford, MR; Bibliothèque Municipale, Dijon, BR/ *Luttrell Psalter*, 1335-40 Add. MS. 42130, f.170/ British Library, London BL. **153** *Chronicle of St. Denis*, Bibliothèque Nationale, Paris/ Bridgeman Art Library, London, T; *Chartres Cathedral from the Great Window, detail of 'The Furriers'*, 13th century/ Sonia Halliday, M; *Women preparing and cutting Linen*, (detail) Italian, 15th century, MS. s.n. 2644, f. 105v, c 1385 /Österreichische Nationalbibliothek, Vienna, BR. **154** British Library, London/ Bridgeman Art Library, TL; *Battle of Crécy*, (detail) French, 15th century/ Bibliothèque Nationale, Paris/ Bridgeman Art Library, London, T; *Annunciation to St. Anne*, fresco by Giotto (detail)/ Scrovegni Chapel, Padua/ Bridgeman Art Library, London, ML; *Anathomia of Guido da Vigevano/ Conde* Museum, Chantilly, B. **155** *Joan of Arc*, (detail) French, 15th century/ Bibliothèque Nationale, Paris/ Bridgeman Art Library, London, TR; *Limbourg Brothers: Les Très Riches Heures du Duc de Berry*, December, 15th century, Victoria & Albert Museum, London/ Bridgeman Art Library, London, ML; *Giovanni Boccaccio: Le Livre de cleres et nobles femmes*, MS. Fr. 12420, f. 86/ Bibliothèque Nationale, Paris, MR; MS. Lat. 8846, f. 106, French, 15th century/ Bibliothèque Nationale, Paris, B.

FRONT COVER: Illustration by Victor Ambrus, TL; Giraudon, ML; British Library, London, M; Museum of London, MR; Robert Harding Picture Library, BL, BR.

BACK COVER: E.T. Archive, TL; British Museum, London, MT; Editions Alecto Limited, TR; British Library, London, M; Illustration by Victor Ambrus, BL; The Bridgeman Art Library, London, BR.